Satura
1962–1970

Also by Eugenio Montale

POETRY

Ossi di seppia (Cuttlefish Bones)
Le occasioni (The Occasions)
La bufera e altro (The Storm and Other Things)
Quaderno di traduzioni (Notebook of Translations)
Diario del '71 e del '72 (Diary of 1971 and 1972)
Quaderno di quattro anni (Notebook of Four Years)
Tutte le poesie (Collected Poems)
L'opera in versi (Poetical Works)
Altri versi e poesie disperse (Other and Uncollected Poems)
Diario postumo (Posthumous Diary)

PROSE

Farfalla di Dinard (Butterfly of Dinard)
Eugenio Montale / Italo Svevo: Lettere con gli scritti di Montale su Svevo
     (The Montale-Svevo Letters, with Montale's writings on Svevo)
Auto da fé: Cronache in due tempi (Act of Faith: Chronicles of Two Periods)
Fuori di casa (Away from Home)
La poesia non esiste (Poetry Doesn't Exist)
Nel nostro tempo (In Our Time)
Sulla poesia (On Poetry)
Lettere a Quasimodo (Letters to Quasimodo)
Prime alla Scala (Openings at La Scala)
Quaderno genovese (Genoa Notebook)

Also by the translator, William Arrowsmith

Satura
1962–1970

Eugenio Montale

Translated with Notes, by

William Arrowsmith

Preface by

Claire de C. L. Huffman

Edited by

Rosanna Warren

W. W. Norton & Company
New York / London

These translations have appeared (some in variant readings) in the following publications: all the poems of *Xenia I* and *Xenia II* in *The Agni Review* (1991); "History," "The Rasp," "Poetry," and "Rhymes" in *Interim* (1987); "To a Modern Jesuit," "La Belle Dame Sans Merci," and "The Archive" in *New England Review* (1997); "In Smoke," "Götterdämmerung," "Fanfare," "Nothing Serious," "Time and Times," "Late at Night," and "Men Who Turn Back" in *Pequod* (1991); "The Black Angel" and "*The Strasbourg cricket drilling away . . .*" in *Shenandoah* (1997); "The Arno at Rovezzano" in *Pequod* (1992); "Tapped Telephone," "Divinity in Disguise," "*From the windows . . .*," "*Farfarella, the gabby doorman . . .*," and "The Other" in *Bostonia* (March–April 1990); "A Month Among Children" and "Ex Voto" in *Passager* (II:3, 1991); "The Euphrates" in *Translation* (1990); "*There were birches . . .*," "*Your gait isn't priest-like . . .*," "*If you'd been ravished . . .*," "*My road made . . .*," "*When I think of you . . .*," "*When we reached Sant'Anna . . .*," "*Slow at accepting neologisms . . .*," "*I can't breathe when you're not here . . .*," and "Piropó, In Conclusion" in *The American Poetry Review* (1991); "Rebecca" in *Partisan Review* (1997); and "In Silence" in *Anataeus* (1990).

Copyright © 1971 by Arnoldo Mondadori Editore SpA
English text copyright © 1998 by The William Arrowsmith Estate and Rosanna Warren
Originally published in Italian

All rights reserved
Printed in the United States of America

For information about permission to reproduce selections from this book, write to Permissions, W. W. Norton & Company, Inc., 500 Fifth Avenue, New York, NY 10110.

The text of this book is composed in Bembo
with the display set in Bembo
Composition by Binghamton Valley Composition.
Manufacturing by the Maple-Vail Book Manufacturing Group

Library of Congress Cataloging-in-Publication Data

Montale, Eugenio, 1896–
[Satura. English]
Satura : 1962–1970 / by Eugenio Montale ; translated with notes,
by William Arrowsmith ; preface by Claire de C.L. Huffman ; edited
by Rosanna Warren.
p.   cm.
ISBN 0-393-04647-8
I. Arrowsmith, William, 1924–   .   II. Warren, Rosanna.
III. Title.
PQ4829.0565S3313   1998   97-32720
851'.912—dc21   CIP

W. W. Norton & Company, Inc., 500 Fifth Avenue, New York, N.Y. 10110
http://www.wwnorton.com

W. W. Norton & Company Ltd., 10 Coptic Street, London WC1A 1PU

1 2 3 4 5 6 7 8 9 0

Contents

SATURA II   69

Editor's Note

When William Arrowsmith died on 20 February 1992, he left in manuscript his translations of every volume of poems by Eugenio Montale arranged by the poet himself, except for *The Storm and Other Things (La bufera e altro)* and *The Occasions (Le occasioni),* which had already appeared from Norton in W. A.'s translation. *Altri versi,* put together for Montale by Giorgio Zampa and published a few months before the poet's death in 1981, was not included; nor, for obvious reasons, was *Diario postumo,* edited by Annalisa Cima and not published *in toto* until 1996. In 1992, Norton brought out, in a posthumous publication, W. A.'s translation of Montale's *Cuttlefish Bones (Ossi di seppia).* Now we can present W. A.'s translation of Montale's volume of poems from 1971, *Satura.* W. A. left far fewer notes for this book than for his previous translations, but I have included the notes because even in their concision they help situate these often obscure poems within Montale's literary, philosophical, and social landscape. At least one of the notes, to "Xenia II, 14," provides an interpretive key to the whole book in its description of the flood in Florence, the *alluvione* that becomes a metaphysical event for Montale as it sweeps away "a part of the mind of Europe." In the notes to "Xenia II, 14" one hears the clear, strong voice of Arrowsmith the critic and interpreter, and one sees at least a sketch of the larger critical work with which he would have accompanied his translation, had time allowed.

Since W. A. did not translate the title, *Satura,* I quote from Joseph Cary. *Satura,* he tells us, is a Latin literary term not to be found in English dictionaries, "a medley, a miscellany, a mixed-dish, a stew, a mélange of attitudes and speech-styles." *Three Modern Italian Poets/Saba, Ungaretti, Montale* (New York: New York University Press, 1969; 2nd ed., Chicago: Chicago University Press, 1993) 360.

In the notes, W. A. uses the following abbreviations:

—E. M. for Eugenio Montale

—SP for Eugenio Montale, *Sulla Poesia* (Milan: Mondadori, 1976)

—Nascimbeni for Giulio Nascimbeni, *Montale: Biografia di un poeta* (Milan: Longanesi Co., 1986)

Notes signed "R. W." were composed by Rosanna Warren.

In preparing the book for publication, I have relied on the careful previous work by W. A.'s assistant, Carrol Hassman; on the patience and diligence of my assistant Joanna Binkowski; and on the moral and literary support offered by Jill Bialosky, Joseph Cary, Claire de C. L. Huffman, Rachel Jacoff, W. S. Di Piero, Christopher Ricks, and Rebecca West. W. A. left the following acknowledgments for *Satura:*

"I am deeply grateful to the painstaking criticism provided by Gertrude Hooker, Simone di Piero, Mack Rosenthal, and Rosanna Warren."

—ROSANNA WARREN

Preface

Eugenio Montale spoke of his fourth volume of poetry, *Satura* (1971), with the same casualness he attributed to its poems, calling it a diaristic, spontaneous collection, different from his earlier works, and bound to disturb those readers and critics who had fixed his place in modern Italian literature. The Nobel Prize–winning poet (1975) had been seen to abide, lastingly, in the tripartite *Ossi di seppia* (1925, *Cuttlefish Bones*), *Le occasioni* (1939, *The Occasions*), and *La bufera e altro* (1956, *The Storm and Other Things*), moving from late Romanticism, naturalism, and isolation *(Ossi),* to the invention of new forms and means of expression, and from these "occasions"—even reasons—for poems to take on shape and to "exist" *(Le occasioni)* to a third great chamber of poetry. This third and "last" was to be the great and myth-filled *La bufera,* where readers felt the presence of Dante, Shakespeare, the English Metaphysical poets, and T. S. Eliot, among others, especially in the richness and intensity of language and emotion. Then Montale immensely enjoyed delivering the surprise—and shock—of *Satura,* inviting the reader to respond variously to its title's connotations of miscellany, satire, and feast.

What Montale did not say—he was, after all, a poet and writer of indirection, irony, and subtlety who abstained from "definition" and refused to direct language "onto" experiences and ideas—and what he must have known, was that *Satura* is a "limit work," a "singular, almost disconcerting text which constitutes at once the secret and the caricature of [the writer's] creation, suggesting thereby the aberrant work [he has] not written . . . and combining a creator's positive and negative aspects."★

Montale had always been on the verge of writing *Satura.* Its voices can be heard in the 1920s. One has only to think of the early correspondence with Italo Svevo, of the self-caricature, the mixed tone and

---

★Roland Barthes, *Critical Essays* (Evanston: Northwestern University Press, 1976) 77.

feelings of his statement to Svevo that his *Ossi* ("bones") are poems best "gnawed on" (letter of 17 March 1927). Much later, when I spoke with and corresponded with Montale in the late 1970s, he frequently compared his role in *Satura* to that of a famous Italian conjurer who invites his audience, after the performance, to see for themselves how he has artfully managed his tricks. *Satura* suggests another Montalian image: that of the "antefacts" behind the stagecraft and stage action of poetry. They must be read in the light of other Montales. Readers of William Arrowsmith's excellent translation of *Satura* will acquaint themselves with the earlier volumes as well if they wish to understand why Montale is often considered to be the most complex and rewarding poet writing in the Italian language since Dante.

Arrowsmith's translation of all Montale meets an urgent need, that of bringing to the English-speaking reader a poet of whom it has been recorded (in the age of statistics) that when compared to Dante's lexicon in the *Commedia (Divine Comedy)*, Montale's has a higher percentage of different words. This type of complexity, together with a conformed sense of Montale's significance, has prompted comparisons, from critics abroad, of Montale with T. S. Eliot and Rainer Maria Rilke, among others, and calls for Montale to be as well known in the United States as he deserves.

Arrowsmith recognized that he was face to face with poetry that continues, at times, to elude even the most deeply attentive critics, at the most basic levels of the text. Many critics have found it difficult to isolate the cohesive elements of Montale's poetry, to define its "thought," to analyze how indefinable emotions rise in previously unexplored areas of poetry, how words may incorporate, bind, and yet barely give up symbolic, phonic, and emotional meanings. Arrowsmith's translations seek to do just this: to reveal Montale's thought and to bind his meanings into English, to highlight the unexpected, to provide a text that corresponds with the original texture of the Italian, especially in its phonic and harmonic complexity.

Earlier, Montale claimed at times to transcribe his poems from an unspoken, unwritten "higher" language, from the unconscious, and from dreams; these inchoate "transcriptions" had, nonetheless, to "pass through" language and meet its semantic demands, to shape inexplicable personal "intentions" and to bow to the finishing touches of technique and artifice.

In isolated passages of the early, great Montale, we find moments, for instance, when infinity, Montale's quested salvation, is suggested by a turn of thought, or by thought turned inward, just hinted at by a play of sound patterns. In "Casa sul mare," for instance, he writes, "Forse solo chi vuole s'infinita, / e questo tu potrai, chissà, non'io." The poet is already discovering a new poetic world where he can touch the eternal ("s'infinita"), deny it ("chissà"), exploit its feeling and its sound ("s'infinita") to bind himself to his poem ("io"), to the recipient other ("chi"), and to obdurate "higher" meanings.

In *Satura* the "transcriptions" take the form of confession, surprise, incandescence, epigram, and internal phonic structuring of details. *Satura* is new in its open, confessional style, its insistently satirical tone and its deliberate playing with the linguistic registers of journalism, diary, and letter, and it is new in its efforts to make poetry where and when poetry seems impossible, in that mood of suspended belief (and disbelief) already expressed in "Botta e risposta I" (1962 [1961]) and in a poetic present time through which pass twin aspects of the poet's past, that which has let itself be turned into poetry and that which continues to resist the process.

Positively, critics have spoken of *Satura*'s [pseudo]-diaristic quality and of newness in a writer whose earlier, tighter work had been compared with Dante and Shakespeare, of a seemingly free poetry, and have pointed to its often unbound contents that leap from poem to poem. Thus the poems can be read all together, at one go, as Montale himself urged, no matter how individually different and miscellaneous they are.

Then, for those who have had the excitement of access to the earlier works, there is the added pleasure of considering *Satura* as (in part) a commentary on the early work—a pleasure not to be underestimated in view of the voluminous criticism that rose nearly overnight in the late 1970s over the earlier three slim volumes. There is novelty; so much so that some have thought of *Satura* as surprisingly avant-garde (for the 1970s in Italy). We hear the "voice" of the elder poet finally speaking out, and sounding "dry" the way Eliot did—an old man in a "dry month." The dryness is strangely rich, not only because Montale leans toward prose and then, out of technical virtuosity, refuses its bounds, but also because he is exploiting simplicity. There is a tendency to understate feelings and ideas; yet everywhere we infer that the poet would have much more to say if only experience were less abrasive, reality less recalcitrant, knowledge less elusive. The "dryness"—like the images of experience—is waiting to be fueled.

Satura is a book of changed questions and ways of asking them. There are fewer abstract entities than earlier in Montale. God is only a felt presence and, more usually, an absence. Time is an empty "now," chronicled and diaried: messages emanate from this "now," fill it, or fail to do so. Often such messages are mere fragments of ideas, barely held onto once, and now broken apart, remnants asking for a higher "language," which is to say, a form of knowledge. The poetic message is intended as final: language is proffered, words offered and withdrawn, bolstered by cultural allusions. The reader is invited to respond to poetic pronouncements with his own understanding. When Montale calls human history a *letamaio* (dunghill) he does so in the hope of being contested. He yields up the decision, choice, and striving to the readers. One metaphor for this late Montale lies in the cultural passage from a fixed religion to a religious stance. We might consider Rudolf Bultmann's paradigms of Christianity falling from its primitive roots into stoicism. In *Primitive Christianity in its Contemporary Setting,* Bultmann writes of the Stoics who have come to believe, with some reservation, that there are things of "no concern of" man, that man's body is alien and the world along with it. In this vision of Stoicism, only desire, will, and imagination are left to man, who is tempted to be free of them as well. Montale has often been termed, latterly, a Stoic, and if he is, this is his form, his stance.

In *Satura* desire seems to be gone, the will broken, and imagination no longer (if ever it was) a binding element in the poetry. Earlier tendencies merge, and again as though on Bultmann's ideal trajectory, the poet moves toward endurance, withdrawal, clarification, and renunciation of tumult and of expectation of the future. The poet, like the would-be Stoic, senses that nothing is new, that one must be armed and that all in all, one must record external reality while shutting one's inner eye to it.

It is not helpful, then, to consider *Satura* as "higher" or "lower" according to the intensity of historical and ideological "messages"; it is more useful to respond to its overtones of irony and denunciation and to relate these to the earlier Montale. Certainly, there has been a loss of belief, for instance in the notion that a series of historical events may yield a truth. In *La bufera* Montale never doubted that forces of good and evil were at war in the 1930s and 40s and that therefore the "real" war was related to a higher Drama. In *Satura,* we get a piling up of details, unassembled into any such idea. There is a stylistic parallel to the ideological (or anti-ideological) strain: one poem flows into another, and images do not agglomerate into the powerful syntagmas and word-auras of the earlier poetry.

For forty-odd years Montale had been revolutionizing language—the Italian language. He was famous for his difficult incandescence, the "miraculism" for which he invented intricate stylistic devices. Through these he could suggest, always, that experience may be transformed into its own message bearer. In *Satura* this transforming process dies away, but because it does not do so entirely we have compensatory humor, ironic withdrawal, and satire. Sergio Solmi has insisted on the humor of the poems. Here is a poet who no longer wants to "show" meanings, since faith itself can only be gotten at, if at all, irrationally. Hence there is an atmosphere of "nothingness," of bodiless voices, whispering in the dark, half-spoken thoughts, often to those already dead and unidentified. There is something, Solmi suggests, quite dark in all of this, something even religious, in the *luce della morte* where the poet sees and (given the particular nature of *Satura*) *re-sees* everything and everyone.

Yet the "earliest" (in published printed order) poem of Montale, "In limine" (1924) the introductory poem to *Ossi,* has, like the poems of *Satura,* similar unity and disunity, flashes of irony, remnants of meanings not organized by the poem, battles between sense and sound, the refusal to appeal to canonized emotions and to canonize the self. From the beginning, too, Montale had proposed that poems can offer no truth or only "minimal" ones, and that the world may yield up only memories and "relics" of meaning.

Rebounding in and among the names, faces, and fact-images of *Satura* (which themselves replace metaphoric activity as the engine of language), are echoes of this "earlier" Montale. The *Ossi* were shocking and surprising, too. They forced Italian readers to accept and to hear (hearing was essential in the new music of *Ossi*) a poetry of suffering and imprisonment, self-declaredly marginal and yet evoking that "other"—image, person, or belief—who may help the poet complete the act of writing and of being. As a translator, Arrowsmith was particularly inspired by this aspect of Montale, by his drive and by his tenacious search, especially in *La bufera,* for any intervention, divine or human, the correlative of which was, at times, the poetry itself, an achieved "compensation."

Every translation represents a gauging of the relative weight of the procedures of the original. In Arrowsmith's *Satura,* one hears a *particular* Montale, in some of his earliest voices, the poet who, in "In limine," thought time a "gag," "joke," and "plot," responded accordingly, and found words for such inventions of feeling. As in *Satura,* in the earlier Montale time weighs upon us and may oppress, filled as much by what is *not* as by what *is.*

But if in an earlier time Montale hoped to change the condition of his mind, his way of seeing, now there is no such ambition, nor is there any need to enshrine the past. What is given is nearly given up. This surrender is challenged by verbal tightness, by an abundance of allusion, and by vitality extracted from verbal and metrical technique.

In choosing this Montale, Arrowsmith grapples with the complex task of translating a poetry which presupposes knowledge of earlier texts and which, at times, overreaches them technically, especially by blending psychological, sound, and "timbric" values (we have word-images, image-sounds, sound-emotions).

Arrowsmith's translation is particularly successful in conveying Montale's unique self-irony. This quality is diffused unevenly throughout *Satura,* often rising unexpectedly, and lurking among images that correspond only indirectly with the poet's way of seeing experience. At times, images are proffered by the others who people his poems, and may have meaning only for these "others," losing them when they touch upon the poet's state of mind, through some failing of memory, or age, or overripeness of knowledge, or skepticism, or lost desire. At times desire remains, but time has worked its "plot." Names have outlasted images, and an overabundance of objects, empty names, and phrases have darkened living memories. The reader becomes the necessary "other" who with the poet will feel the limitations of today's words and will listen instead to what is not exactly said in *Satura.*

Montale herein continues his poetic revolution. In the original texts, and not only in *Satura,* vowels are often played upon to give the texture of a thought or of a feeling. At times words are proffered and then withheld. Under such circumstances, it has often been said of Montale that not a single word or sound can be taken for granted, not even a conjunction. (Italian critics who have tried to make Montale accessible to uninitiated Italian readers have had difficulty "translating" Montale into the Italian of commentary and paraphrase!) In such poetry there is nothing indifferent. Complexity of allusion and subtlety of image will send the reader to Arrowsmith's useful notes.

Arrowsmith was passionately devoted to all of Montale, interested, above all, in retaining the "strangeness" and "otherness" of his poetic language which, as George Steiner has pointed out in *After Babel,* is largely the purpose of translation. This translation of *Satura* is also an "homage," what John Felstiner (in the foreword to *Paul Celan: Poet, Survivor, Jew,* his translation of Paul Celan) called the convergence of "critical and creative activity," so that translation presents not merely a paradigm but the utmost case of engaged literary interpretation.

—CLAIRE DE C. L. HUFFMAN
Brooklyn College, CUNY

My you

I critici ripetono,
da me depistati,
che il mio tu è un istituto.
Senza questa mia colpa avrebbero saputo
che in me i tanti sono uno anche se appaiono
moltiplicati dagli specchi. Il male
è che l'uccello preso nel paretaio
non sa se lui sia lui o uno dei troppi
suoi duplicati.

Misled by me,
the critics keep on saying
that my you *is standard practice.*
If not for this foible of mine, they would have known
that in me the many are one, though seemingly
multiplied by mirrors. The problem
is that of the netted bird
who doesn't know whether he's trapped
or it's one of his too many doubles.

Botta e risposta I

I

«Arsenio» (lei mi scrive), «io qui 'asolante'
tra i miei tetri cipressi penso che
sia ora di sospendere la tanto
da te per me voluta sospensione
d'ogni inganno mondano; che sia tempo
di spiegare le vele e di sospendere
l'*epoché*.

Non dire che la stagione è nera ed anche le tortore
con le tremule ali sono volate al sud.
Vivere di memorie non posso più.
Meglio il morso del ghiaccio che il tuo torpore
di sonnambulo, o tardi risvegliato».

(lettera da Asolo)

II

Uscito appena dall'adolescenza
per metà della vita fui gettato
nelle stalle d'Augìa.

Non vi trovai duemila bovi, né
mai vi scorsi animali;
pure nei corridoi, sempre più folti
di letame, si camminava male
e il respiro mancava; ma vi crescevano
di giorno in giorno i muggiti umani.

Thrust and Parry I

I

"Arsenio" (she writes me), "here, *asolando*
among my gloomy cypresses, I think
it's time to suspend
that suspension of every worldly illusion
you so much wanted for me; time
to unfurl the sails and suspend
the *epoché*.

Stop saying the weather's foul and even the doves
with shivering wings have flown south.
I can't go on living with memories.
Better the bite of ice than your sleepwalker's
torpor, or late awakening."

(letter from Asolo)

II

Barely out of adolescence
I was thrown for half my life
into the Augean stables.

I didn't find two thousand oxen, and I never
spotted any animals there;
but it was hard going and bad breathing
even in the corridors, dung everywhere
and always more and more; there, day by day
the human bellowing grew louder.

Lui non fu mai veduto.
La geldra però lo attendeva
per il presentat-arm: stracolmi imbuti,
forconi e spiedi, un'infilzata fetida
di saltimbocca. Eppure
non una volta Lui sporse
cocca di manto o punta di corona
oltre i bastioni d'ebano, fecali.

Poi d'anno in anno—e chi più contava
le stagioni in quel buio?—qualche mano
che tentava invisibili spiragli
insinuò il suo memento: un ricciolo
di Gerti, un grillo in gabbia, ultima traccia
del transito di Liuba, il microfilm
d'un sonetto eufuista scivolato
dalle dita di Clizia addormentata,
un ticchettìo di zoccoli (la serva
zoppa di Monghidoro)
                              finché dai cretti
il ventaglio di un mitra ci ributtava,
badilanti infiacchiti colti in fallo
dai bargelli del brago.

Ed infine fu il tonto: l'incredibile.

A liberarci, a chiuder gli intricati
cunicoli in un lago, bastò un attimo
allo stravolto Alfeo. Chi l'attendeva
ormai? Che senso aveva quella nuova
palta? e il respirare altre ed eguali
zaffate? e il vorticare sopra zattere
di sterco? ed era sole quella sudicia
esca di scolaticcio sui fumaioli,
erano uomini forse,
veri uomini vivi
i formiconi degli approdi?

                . . . .

He was never seen.
Yet the rabble kept expecting Him
for the present arms: funnels overflowing,
forks and spits, skewers of rotten
saltimbocca. And yet
not once did He extend
the hem of his robe or show a tip of His crown
outside the bastions of fecal ebony.

Then, year after year—who in that darkness
could keep count of the seasons?—a few hands
groping for invisible chinks
inserted their mementos—one of Gerti's
curls, a cricket in a cage, last trace
of Liuba's journey, the microfilm
of a euphuistic sonnet that slipped
from the fingers of Clizia sleeping,
the clatter of clogs (the limping maid
from Monghidoro)
                    until, fanning from the slits,
a burst of machine-gun fire hurled us back,
drooping ditchdiggers accidentally caught
by the dunghill guards.

And finally came the thud: the incredible.

Liberating us, sealing the mazes
of that hellish warren in a lake, was an instant's work
for the diverted Alpheus. Who expected Him
now? What was the meaning of that new
muck? And the different but no less sickening
stench exhaled? And the wild gyring of shit
over the barges? And was that the sun, that sweaty
lure of slag and dregs on the smokestacks,
could those be men,
real living men,
those huge ants on the beachheads?

· ·

                              (Penso
che forse non mi leggi più. Ma ora
tu sai tutto di me,
della mia prigionia e del mio dopo;
ora sai che non può nascere l'aquila
dal topo).

                              (I think
you may have stopped reading me. But now
you know everything about me,
about my imprisonment and the aftermath;
now you know the eagle isn't sired
by the mouse).

Xenia I

1

Caro piccolo insetto
che chiamavano mosca non so perché,
stasera quasi al buio
mentre leggevo il Deuteroisaia
sei ricomparsa accanto a me,
ma non avevi occhiali,
non potevi vedermi
né potevo io senza quel luccichìo
riconoscere te nella foschia.

2

Senza occhiali né antenne,
povero insetto che ali
avevi solo nella fantasia,
una bibbia sfasciata ed anche poco
attendibile, il nero della notte,
un lampo, un tuono e poi
neppure la tempesta. Forse che
te n'eri andata così presto senza
parlare? Ma è ridicolo
pensare che tu avessi ancora labbra.

3

Al Saint James di Parigi dovrò chiedere
una camera 'singola'. (Non amano
i clienti spaiati). E così pure
nella falsa Bisanzio del tuo albergo
veneziano; per poi cercare subito
lo sgabuzzino delle telefoniste,
le tue amiche di sempre; e ripartire,
esaurita la carica meccanica,
il desiderio di riaverti, fosse
pure in un solo gesto o un'abitudine.

1

Dear little insect
nicknamed Mosca, I don't know why,
this evening, when it was nearly dark,
while I was reading Deutero-Isaiah,
you reappeared at my side,
but without your glasses
you couldn't see me,
and in the blur, without their glitter,
I didn't know who you were.

2

Minus glasses and antennae,
poor insect, wingèd
only in imagination,
a beaten-up Bible and none
too reliable either, black night,
a flash of lightning, thunder, and then
not even the storm. Could it be
you left so soon, without
a word? But it's crazy, my thinking
you still had lips.

3

At the St. James in Paris I'll have to ask for
a room for one. (They don't like
single guests.) Ditto
in the fake Byzantium of your Venetian
hotel; and then, right off, hunting down
the girls at the switchboard,
always your pals; and then leaving again
the minute my three minutes are up,
and the wanting you back,
if only in one gesture,
one habit of yours.

4

Avevamo studiato per l'aldilà
un fischio, un segno di riconoscimento.
Mi provo a modularlo nella speranza
che tutti siamo già morti senza saperlo.

5

Non ho mai capito se io fossi
il tuo cane fedele e incimurrito
o tu lo fossi per me.
Per gli altri no, eri un insetto miope
smarrito nel blabla
dell'alta società. Erano ingenui
quei furbi e non sapevano
di essere loro il tuo zimbello:
di esser visti anche al buio e smascherati
da un tuo senso infallibile, dal tuo
radar di pipistrello.

6

Non hai pensato mai di lasciar traccia
di te scrivendo prosa o versi. E fu
il tuo incanto—e dopo la mia nausea di me.
Fu pure il mio terrore: di esser poi
ricacciato da te nel gracidante
limo dei neòteroi.

7

Pietà di sé, infinita pena e angoscia
di chi adora il quaggiù e spera e dispera
di un altro . . . (Chi osa dire un altro mondo?).
. . . .

'Strana pietà . . . ' (*Azucena*, atto secondo).

4

We'd worked out a whistle for the world
beyond, a token of recognition.
Now I'm trying variations, hoping
we're all dead already and don't know it.

5

I've never figured out whether I
was your faithful dog with runny eyes
or you were mine.
To others you were a myopic little bug
bewildered by the twaddle
of high society. They were naive,
those catty folk, never guessing
they were the butt of your humor:
that you could see them even in the dark,
unmasked by your infallible sixth sense,
your bat's radar.

6

You never thought of leaving your mark
by writing prose or verse. This
was your charm—and later my self-revulsion.
It was what I dreaded too: that someday
you'd shove me back into the croaking
bog of modern neoterics.

7

Self-pity, infinite pain and anguish
of the man who worships this world here and now,
who hopes and despairs of another . . .
(who dares speak of another world?)

. . . .

"Strana pietà . . ." (*Azucena,* Act II)

8

La tua parola così stenta e imprudente
resta la sola di cui mi appago.
Ma è mutato l'accento, altro il colore.
Mi abituerò a sentirti o a decifrarti
nel ticchettìo della telescrivente,
nel volubile fumo dei miei sigari
di Brissago.

9

Ascoltare era il solo tuo modo di vedere.
Il conto del telefono s'è ridotto a ben poco.

10

«Pregava?». «Sì, pregava Sant'Antonio
perché fa ritrovare
gli ombrelli smarriti e altri oggetti
del guardaroba di Sant'Ermete».
«Per questo solo?». «Anche per i suoi morti
e per me».
　　　　　«È sufficient» disse il prete.

11

Ricordare il tuo pianto (il mio era doppio)
non vale a spenger lo scoppio delle tue risate.
Erano come l'anticipo di un tuo privato
Giudizio Universale, mai accaduto purtroppo.

12

La primavera sbuca col suo passo di talpa.
Non ti sentirò più parlare di antibiotici
velenosi, del chiodo del tuo femore,
dei beni di fortuna che t'ha un occhiuto omissis
spennacchiati.

8

Your speech so halting and tactless
is the only speech that consoles me.
But the tone has changed, the color too.
I'll get used to hearing you, decoding you
in the click-clack of the teletype,
in the spirals of smoke coiling
from my Brissago cigars.

9

Listening was your only way of seeing.
The phone bill comes to almost nothing now.

10

"Did she pray?" "Yes to St. Anthony
who's in charge of finding lost
umbrellas and suchlike things
in St. Hermes' cloakroom."
"And that's it?" "She prayed for her dead too,
and for me."
                    "Quite enough," the priest replied.

11

The memory of your tears (I cried twice as hard)
can't obliterate your wild peals of laughter.
They were a kind of foretaste
of a private Last Judgment of your own,
which, alas, never came to pass.

12

Spring pokes out at a snail's pace.
Never again will I hear you talking of antibiotic
poisoning, or the pin in your femur;
or the patrimony plucked from you
by that thousand-eyed
[deleted].

La primavera avanza con le sue nebbie grasse,
con le sue luci lunghe, le sue ore insopportabili.
Non ti sentirò più lottare col rigurgito
del tempo, dei fantasmi, dei problemi logistici
dell'Estate.

13

Tuo fratello morì giovane; tu eri
la bimba scarruffata che mi guarda
'in posa' nell'ovale di un ritratto.
Scrisse musiche inedite, inaudite,
oggi sepolte in un baule o andate
al màcero. Forse le riinventa
qualcuno inconsapevole, se ciò ch'è scritto è scritto.
L'amavo senza averlo conosciuto.
Fuori di te nessuno lo ricordava.
Non ho fatto ricerche: ora è inutile.
Dopo di te sono rimasto il solo
per cui egli è esistito. Ma è possibile,
lo sai, amare un'ombra, ombre noi stessi.

14

Dicono che la mia
sia una poesia d'inappartenenza.
Ma s'era tua era di qualcuno:
di te che non sei più forma, ma essenza.
Dicono che la poesia al suo culmine
magnifica il Tutto in fuga,
negano che la testuggine
sia più veloce del fulmine.
Tu sola sapevi che il moto
non è diverso dalla stasi,
che il vuoto è il pieno e il sereno
è la più diffusa delle nubi.
Così meglio intendo il tuo lungo viaggio
imprigionata tra le bende e i gessi.
Eppure non mi dà riposo
sapere che in uno o in due noi siamo una sola cosa.

Spring comes on with its heavy fogs,
long daylights and unbearable hours.
Never again will I hear you struggling with the backwash
of time, or ghosts, or the logistical problems
of summer.

13

Your brother died young; that little girl
with tousled curls in the oval portrait,
looking at me, was you.
He wrote music, unpublished, unheard,
now buried away in some trunk
or trashed. If what's written is written,
maybe someone, unawares, is rewriting it now.
I loved him without ever knowing him.
Except for you no one remembered him.
I made no inquiries; it's futile now.
After you, I was the only one left
for whom he ever existed.
But we can love a shade, you know,
being shades ourselves.

14

They say my poetry is one of nonbelonging.
But if it was yours, it was someone's:
it was yours who are no longer form, but essence.
They say that poetry at its peak
glorifies the All in flight,
they say the tortoise
is no swifter than lightning.
You alone knew
that movement and stasis are one,
that the void is fullness and the clear sky
cloud at its airiest. So your long journey,
imprisoned by bandages and casts,
makes better sense to me.
Still, knowing we're a single thing,
whether one or two, gives me no peace.

Xenia II

1

La morte non ti riguardava.
Anche i tuoi cani erano morti, anche
il medico dei pazzi detto lo zio demente,
anche tua madre e la sua 'specialità'
di riso e rane, trionfo meneghino;
e anche tuo padre che da una minieffigie
mi sorveglia dal muro sera e mattina.
Malgrado ciò la morte non ti riguardava.

Ai funerali dovevo andare io,
nascosto in un tassì restandone lontano
per evitare lacrime e fastidi. E neppure
t'importava la vita e le sue fiere
di vanità e ingordige e tanto meno le
cancrene universali che trasformano
gli uomini in lupi

Una tabula rasa; se non fosse
che un punto c'era, per me incomprensibile,
e questo punto *ti riguardava.*

2

Spesso ti ricordavi (io poco) del signor Cap.
«L'ho visto nel torpedone, a Ischia, appena due volte.
È un avvocato di Klagenfurt, quello che manda gli auguri.
Doveva venirci a torvare».

E infine è venuto, gli dico tutto, resta imbambolato,
pare che sia una catastrofe anche per lui. Tace a lungo,
farfuglia, s'alza rigido e s'inchina. Conferma
che manderà gli auguri.
                        È strano che a comprenderti
siano riuscite solo persone inverosimili.
Il dottor Cap! Basta il nome. E Celia? Che n'è accaduto?

I

For you death didn't matter.
Your dogs had died, and so had the asylum
doctor nicknamed "Uncle Bonkers,"
and your mother and her "speciality,"
risotto with frogs' legs, a Milanese triumph;
and your father looking down on me
day and night from his mini-likeness on the wall.
Despite all this, for you death didn't matter.

It was I who had to attend the funerals—
hidden in a taxi, keeping my distance
to avoid tears and fussing. Even life
with its vanity fairs and greed
was no great matter, and the universal gangrenes
that transform men into wolves
didn't much matter.

A tabula rasa; except
for one point, incomprehensible to me,
and *for you* this point *did matter.*

2

You often (I seldom) recalled Mr. Cap.
"I met him, once or twice, in the bus at Ischia.
He's a lawyer from Klagenfurt, who sends us greetings.
He was supposed to come calling."

And finally he came. I tell him the whole story, he's flabbergasted:
for him too it seems a catastrophe. For a moment he's speechless,
then mumbles, rises stiffly, and bows. He assures me
he'll send you his regards.
                              Strange that only
quite improbable people managed to understand you.
Dr. Cap! The name's enough. And Celia? Whatever became of Celia?

3

L'abbiamo rimpianto a lungo l'infilascarpe,
il cornetto di latta arrugginito ch'era
sempre con noi. Pareva un'indecenza portare
tra i similori e gli stucchi un tale orrore.
Dev'essere al Danieli che ho scordato
di riporlo in valigia o nel sacchetto
Hedia la cameriera lo buttò certo
nel Canalazzo. E come avrei potuto
scrivere che cercassero quel pezzaccio di latta?
C'era un prestigio (il nostro) da salvare
e Hedia, la fedele, l'aveva fatto.

4

Con astuzia,
uscendo dalle fauci di Mongibello
o da dentiere di ghiaccio
rivelavi incredibili agnizioni.

Se ne avvide Mangàno, il buon cerusico,
quando, disoccultato, fu il randello
delle camicie nere e ne sorrise.

Così eri: anche sul ciglio del crepaccio
dolcezza e orrore in una sola musica.

5

Ho sceso, dandoti il braccio, almeno un milione di scale
e ora che non ci sei è il vuoto ad ogni gradino.
Anche così è stato breve il nostro lungo viaggio.
Il mio dura tuttora, né più mi occorrono
le coincidenze, le prenotazioni,
le trappole, gli scorni di chi crede
che la realtà sia quella che si vede.

3

For weeks we mourned the lost shoehorn,
the rusty tin shoehorn we took with us
everywhere. It seemed indecent, lugging
junk like that into a world of pinchbeck and stuccoes.
At the Danieli I must have forgotten
to slip it into the suitcase or satchel,
and the chambermaid, Hedia, probably tossed it
into the Grand Canal. And how could I have written
asking them to look for that hideous tin gizmo?
Prestige (ours) was at stake
and the faithful Hedia had preserved it.

4

Cunningly
emerging from Mongibello's jaws
or fangs of ice,
you arranged incredible recognition-scenes.

The good surgeon Mangàno noticed it
when you unmasked him as the billy club of the Blackshirts,
and he smiled.

Just like you: even on the edge of the precipice
sweetness and horror fused in a single music.

5

Your arm in mine, I've descended a million stairs at least,
and now that you're not here, a void yawns at every step.
Even so our long journey was brief.
I'm still en route, with no further need
of reservations, connections, ruses,
the constant contempt of those who think reality
is what one sees.

Ho sceso milioni di scale dandoti il braccio
non già perché con quattr'occhi forse si vede di più.
Con te le ho scese perché sapevo che di noi due
le sole vere pupille, sebbene tanto offuscate,
erano le tue.

6

Il vinattiere ti versava un poco
d'Inferno. E tu, atterrita: «Devo berlo? Non basta
esserci stati dentro a lento fuoco?».

7

«Non sono mai stato certo di essere al mondo».
«Bella scoperta, m'hai risposto, e io?».
«Oh il mondo tu l'hai mordicchiato, se anche
in dosi omeopatiche. Ma io . . . ».

8

«E il Paradiso? Esiste un paradiso?».
«Credo di sì, signora, ma i vini dolci
non li vuol più nessuno».

9

Le monache e le vedove, mortifere
maleodoranti prefiche,
non osavi guardarle. Lui stesso che ha mille occhi,
li distoglie da loro, n'eri certa.
L'onniveggente, lui . . . perché tu, giudiziosa,
dio non lo nominavi neppure con la minuscola.

10

Dopo lunghe ricerche
ti trovai in un bar dell'Avenida
da Liberdade; non sapevi un'acca
di portoghese o meglio una parola

I've descended millions of stairs giving you my arm,
not of course because four eyes see better.
I went downstairs with you because I knew
the only real eyes, however darkened,
belonged to you.

6

The wine peddler poured you a thimble
of Inferno. And you, shrinking back: "Must I drink it?
Isn't it enough to simmer in the stuff?"

7

"I've never been certain of being in the world."
"A fine discovery," you replied, "what about me?"
"Oh, you nibbled at the world, even though
the doses were homeopathic. Whereas I . . ."

8

"And Paradise? Is there a paradise too?"
"I think so, Signora, but nobody likes
those sweet dessert wines anymore."

9

Nuns and widows, the plague
of foul-smelling hired mourners—
you didn't dare look at them. The Argus-eyed himself,
you were sure, averts his eyes.
The all-seeing one himself . . . since you were scrupulous
about not calling him god, not even lowercase.

10

After long searching
I found you in a bar on the Avenida
da Libertade; you didn't know a scrap
of Portuguese, or rather just one

sola: Madeira. E venne il bicchierino
con un contorno di aragostine.

La sera fui paragonato ai massimi
lusitani dai nomi impronunciabili
e al Carducci in aggiunta.
Per nulla impressionata io ti vedevo piangere
dal ridere nascosta in una folla
forse annoiata ma compunta.

11

Riemersa da un'infinità di tempo
Celia la filippina ha telefonato
per aver tue notizie. Credo stia bene, dico,
forse meglio di prima. «Come, crede?
Non ce'è più?». Forse più di prima, ma . . .
Celia, cerchi d'intendere . . .
                              Di là dal filo
da Manila o da altra
parola dell'atlante una balbuzie
impediva anche lei. E riagganciò di scatto.

12

I falchi
sempre troppo lontani dal tuo sguardo
raramente li hai visti davvicino.
Uno a Étretat che sorvegliava i goffi
voli dei suoi bambini.
Due altri in Grecia, sulla via di Delfi,
una zuffa di piume soffici, due becchi giovani
arditi e inoffensivi.

Ti piaceva la vita fatta a pezzi,
quella che rompe dal suo insopportabile
ordito.

word: Madeira. And the little glass
arrived, garnished with shrimp.

That evening they compared me to the greatest
Lusitanians with unpronounceable names
and also to Carducci.
I glimpsed you hiding in the crowd,
weeping with laughter, utterly unimpressed,
bored perhaps but feigning admiration.

11

Surfacing from an infinity of time,
Celia phoned from the Philippines
for news of you. She's well, I guess,
maybe better off than before. "What do you mean, you guess?
She's not there anymore?" Maybe more than before, but . . .
Celia, try to understand . . .
                                        From the other end,
from Manila or some other placename
on the map a stammering
stopped her too. And she hung up, abruptly.

12

Hawks
always beyond your range of vision,
you almost never saw them close up.
There was one at Étretat, keeping an eye
on the gawky flights of its fledglings.
Two more in Greece, on the road to Delphi,
a scuffling of downy feathers, two young beaks,
feisty and harmless.

You liked life torn to shreds,
life breaking free of its unbearable
web.

13

Ho appeso nella mia stanza il dagherròtipo
di tuo padre bambino: ha più di un secolo.
In mancanza del mio, così confuso,
cerco di ricostruire, ma invano, il tuo pedigree.
Non siamo stati cavalli, i dati dei nostri ascendenti
non sono negli almanacchi. Coloro che hanno presunto
di saperne non erano essi stessi esistenti,
né noi per loro. E allora? Eppure resta
che qualcosa è accaduto, forse un niente
che è tutto.

14

L'alluvione ha sommerso il pack dei mobili,
delle carte, dei quadri che stipavano
un sotterraneo chiuso a doppio lucchetto.
Forse hanno ciecamente lottato i marocchini
rossi, le sterminate dediche di Du Bos,
il timbro a ceralacca con la barba di Ezra,
il Valéry di Alain, l'originale
dei Canti Orfici—e poi qualche pennello
da barba, mille cianfrusaglie e tutte
le musiche di tuo fratello Silvio.
Dieci, dodici giorni sotto un'atroce morsura
di nafta e sterco. Certo hanno sofferto
tanto prima di perdere la loro identità.
Anch'io sono incrostato fino al collo se il mio
stato civile fu dubbio fin dall'inizio.
Non torba m'ha assediato, ma gli eventi
di una realtà incredibile e mai creduta.
Di fronte ad essi il mio coraggio fu il primo
dei tuoi prestiti e forse non l'hai saputo.

13

In my room I hung the daguerreotype
of your father as a boy; it's more than a century old.
At a loss, having no pedigree of my own,
I try reconstructing yours, to no avail.
We weren't horses, there are no data on our forebears
in the studbooks. Those who presumed to know
the facts had no existence themselves,
nor we for them. And so? Still, it's a fact
that something happened, maybe a nothing
which is everything.

14

The flood has drowned the clutter
of furniture, papers, and paintings that crammed
the double-padlocked cellar.
Maybe they fought back blindly—the books
in red morocco, Du Bos's endless dedications,
the wax seal with Ezra's beard, Alain's
Valéry, the manuscript
of the Orphic Songs, as well as a couple
of shaving brushes, a thousand knickknacks, and all
your brother Silvio's compositions.
Ten, twelve days in that savage maw
of fuel oil and shit. Clearly they suffered
terribly before losing their identity.
I'm deep in crud too, up to my neck, though
my civil status was doubtful from the outset.
It's not muck that besets me, but the events
of an unbelievable, and always unbelieved, reality.
My courage in facing it was the first
of your loans, and perhaps you never knew.

Satura I

Gerarchie

La polis è più importante delle sue parti.
La parte è più importante d'ogni sua parte.
Il predicato lo è più del predicante
e l'arrestato lo è meno dell'arrestante.

Il tempo s'infutura nel totale,
il totale è il cascame del totalizzante,
l'avvento è l'improbabile nell'avvenibile,
il pulsante una pulce nel pulsabile.

Hierarchies

The polis is more important than its parts.
The part is more important than the sum of its parts.
The predicate is more than the predicant,
and the arrested less than the arrester.

Time is enfutured in the total,
the total's the residue of the totalizing,
the advent the improbable in the advenient,
the button a bug in the doorbell.

Déconfiture non vuol dire che la crème caramel
uscita dallo stampo non stia in piedi.
Vuol dire altro disastro; ma per noi sconsacrati
e non mai confettati può bastare.

Déconfiture doesn't mean the crème caramel
collapses on leaving the mold. It means
a different kind of disaster; but for folk like us,
uncomfited, unchurched, disaster enough.

La storia

I

La storia non si snoda
come una catena
di anelli ininterrotta.
In ogni caso
molti anelli non tengono.
La storia non contiene
il prima e il dopo,
nulla che in lei borbotti
a lento fuoco.
La storia non è prodotta
da chi la pensa e neppure
da chi l'ignora. La storia
non si fa strada, si ostina,
detesta il poco a poco, non procede
né recede, si sposta di binario
e la sua direzione
non è nell'orario.
La storia non giustifica
e non deplora,
la storia non è intrinseca
perché è fuori.
La storia non somministra
carezze o colpi di frusta.
La storia non è magistra
di niente che ci riguardi.
Accorgersene non serve
a farla più vera e più giusta.

History

I

History isn't flexible
like an unbroken
link chain.
In any case
many links don't hold.
History has
no before and after,
nothing in it simmers
on a slow fire.
History isn't made
by its students, not even by those
who know nothing about it. History
doesn't progress, it digs in its heels,
it loathes the gradual, neither advances
nor regresses, it changes tracks
and its course
has no timetable.
History neither justifies
nor blames;
being external,
history isn't intrinsic.
History administers
neither kind words nor whippings.
History is no teacher
of anything that concerns us.
Awareness of this doesn't make it
more true, more just.

II

La storia non è poi
la devastante ruspa che si dice.
Lascia sottopassaggi, cripte, buche
e nascondigli. C'è chi sopravvive.
La storia è anche benevola: distrugge
quanto più può: se esagerasse, certo
sarebbe meglio, ma la storia è a corto
di notizie, non compie tutte le sue vendette.

La storia gratta il fondo
come una rete a strascico
con qualche strappo e più di un pesce sfugge.
Qualche volta s'incontra l'ectoplasma
d'uno scampato e non sembra particolarmente felice.
Ignora di essere fuori, nessuno glie n'ha parlato.
Gli altri, nel sacco, si credono
più liberi di lui.

II

So history is not
the destructive steam shovel it's said to be,
leaving tunnels, crypts, manholes,
hiding-places behind. Some survive it.
History is benevolent too, destroying
what it can: better of course
if more were destroyed, but history is short
on information and long on vendettas.

History scrapes the bottom
like a dragnet periodically
hauled in. A few fish escape,
and at times you meet the ectoplasm
of a survivor, and he doesn't seem specially happy.
He's unaware he's free, nobody's told him.
The others, those in the net, think they're
more free than he.

In vetrina

Gli uccelli di malaugurio
gufi o civette vivono soltanto
in casbe denutrite o imbalsamati
nelle bacheche dei misantropi. Ora
potrebbe anche accadere che la rondine
nidifichi in un tubo e un imprudente
muoia per asfissia. È un incidente
raro e non muta il quadro.

In the Showcase

Birds of ill-omen
owls large and small live only
in starveling slums or stuffed
in the showcases of misanthropes. Now
the swallow—maybe she
nested in a pipe and a brash male
got asphyxiated. It seldom happens
and it doesn't change the picture.

Il raschino

Credi che il pessimismo
sia davvero esistito? Se mi guardo
d'attorno non ne è traccia.
Dentro di noi, poi, non una voce
che si lagni. Se piango è un controcanto
per arricchire il grande
paese di cuccagna ch'è il domani.
Abbiamo ben grattato col raschino
ogni eruzione del pensiero. Ora
tutti i colori esaltano la nostra tavolozza,
escluso il nero.

The Rasp

You think pessimism
ever really existed? I can't see
a sign of it anywhere.
Within us, then, not a single
complaining voice. If I gripe,
it's a countersong to enrich that great
Land of Cockaigne which is Tomorrow.
With our rasp we've scraped away
every eruption of thought. Now
all colors enhance our palette,
all but black.

La morte di Dio

Tutte le religioni del Dio unico
sono una sola: variano i cuochi e le cotture.
Così rimuginavo; e m'interruppi quando
tu scivolasti vertiginosamente
dentro la scala a chiocciola della Périgourdine
e di laggiù ridesti a crepapelle.
Fu una buona serata con un attimo appena
di spavento. Anche il papa
in Israele disse la stessa cosa
ma se ne pentì quando fu informato
che il sommo Emarginato, se mai fu,
era perento.

The Death of God

All religions of the one God
are only one, cooks and cooking vary.
I was turning this thought over
when you interrupted me
by tumbling head-over-heels
down the spiral staircase of the Périgourdine
and at the bottom split your sides laughing.
A delightful evening, marred only by a moment's
fright. Even the pope
in Israel said the same thing
but repented when informed
that the supreme Deposed, if he ever existed,
had expired.

A un gesuita moderno

Paleontologo e prete, ad abundantiam
uomo di mondo, se vuoi farci credere
che un sentore di noi si stacchi dalla crosta
di quaggiù, meno crosta che paniccia,
per allogarsi poi nella noosfera
che avvolge le altre sfere o è in condominio
e sta nel tempo (!),
ti dirò che la pelle mi si aggriccia
quando ti ascolto. Il tempo non conclude
perché non è neppure incominciato.
È neonato anche Dio. A noi di farlo
vivere o farne senza; a noi di uccidere
il tempo perché in lui non è possibile
l'esistenza.

To a Modern Jesuit

Paleontologist and priest, man-of-the-world
ad abundantiam, if you want to persuade us
that some whiff of us separates from the crust
down below—more dough than crust—
to take up lodgings in the noosphere
that surrounds the other spheres or shares their dominion
and exists in time (!),
I'll tell you I get goose bumps
just hearing you talk. Time doesn't end
because it hasn't even begun.
God's a newborn too. It's our job
to make him live or do without him; our job to kill time
since for him existence in time
is impossible.

Nel fumo

Quante volte t'ho atteso alla stazione
nel freddo, nella nebbia. Passeggiavo
tossicchiando, comprando giornali innominabili,
fumando Giuba poi soppresse dal ministro
dei tabacchi, il balordo!
Forse un treno sbagliato, un doppione oppure una
sottrazione. Scrutavo le carriole
dei facchini se mai ci fosse dentro
il tuo bagaglio, e tu dietro, in ritardo.
Poi apparivi, ultima. È un ricordo
tra tanti altri. Nel sogno mi perseguita.

In Smoke

How many times in cold and fog I've waited
for you at the station. I'd pace up and down,
coughing, buying unmentionable newspapers,
smoking Giuba cigarettes (their sale later suspended
by the airhead Minister of Tobacco).
Maybe a missed or an extra train, or just plain
cancelled. I'd inspect the porters'
carts to see if maybe your suitcase
were there, and you lagging behind.
Then, last of all, you appeared. One memory
among so many. It dogs me in my dreams.

Götterdämmerung

Si legge che il crepuscolo degli Dei
stia per incominciare. È un errore.
Gli inizi sono sempre inconoscibili,
se si accerta un qualcosa, quello è già
trafitto dallo spillo.
Il crepuscolo è nato quando l'uomo
si è creduto più degno di una talpa o di un grillo.
L'inferno che si ripete è appena l'anteprova
di una 'prima assoluta' da tempo rimandata
perché il regista è occupato, è malato, imbucato
chissà dove e nessuno può sostituirlo.

Götterdämmerung

We read that the twilight of the gods
is about to begin. A mistake.
Beginnings are always unrecognizable;
when an event is verified, it's been spotted before.
Twilight began when man thought
himself of greater dignity than moles or crickets.
A self-repeating hell is hardly the tryout
of a "grande première" long postponed
because the director's busy, sick, holed up
who knows where, and no one can sub for him.

Intercettazione telefonica

Credevo di essere un vescovo
in partibus
(non importa la parte
purché disabitata)
ma fui probabilmente cardinale
in pectore
senza esserne informato.
Anche il papa morendo
s'è scordato di dirlo.
Posso così vivere nella gloria
(per quel che vale) con fede o senza fede
e in qualsiasi paese
ma fuori della storia
e in abito borghese.

Tapped Telephone

I thought I was a bishop
in partibus
(no matter where
so long as it's uninhabited)
but I was probably a cardinal
in pectore
without being informed.
Even the pope when dying
forgot to mention it.
So I can live in glory
(for what that's worth) with or without
faith, and in any country whatever
but outside of history
and in mufti.

La poesia

I

L'angosciante questione
se sia a freddo o a caldo l'ispirazione
non appartiene alla scienza termica.
Il raptus non produce, il vuoto non conduce,
non c'è poesia al sorbetto o al girarrosto.
Si tratterà piuttosto di parole
molto importune
che hanno fretta di uscire
dal forno o dal surgelante.
Il fatto non è importante. Appena fuori
si guardano d'attorno e hanno l'aria di dirsi:
che sto a farci?

II

Con orrore
la poesia rifiuta
le glosse degli scoliasti.
Ma non è certo che la troppo muta
basti a se stessa
o al trovarobe che in lei è inciampato
senza sapere di esserne
l'autore.

Poetry

I

The agonizing question
whether inspiration is hot or cold
is not a matter of thermodynamics.
Raptus doesn't produce, the void doesn't conduce,
there's no poetry à la sorbet or barbecued.
It's more a matter of very
importunate words
rushing
from oven or deep freeze.
The source doesn't matter. No sooner are they out
than they look around and seem to be saying:
What am I doing here?

II

Poetry
rejects with horror
the glosses of commentators.
But it's unclear that the excessively mute
is sufficient unto itself
or to the property man who's stumbled onto it,
unaware that he's
the author.

Le rime

Le rime sono più noiose delle
dame di San Vincenzo: battono alla porta
e insistono. Respingerle è impossibile
e purché stiano fuori si sopportano.
Il poeta decente le allontana
(le rime), le nasconde, bara, tenta
il contrabbando. Ma le pinzochere ardono
di zelo e prima o poi (rime e vecchiarde)
bussano ancora e sono sempre quelle.

Rhymes

Rhymes are pests, worse
than the nuns of St. Vincent, knocking at your door
nonstop. You can't just turn them away
and they're tolerable so long as they're outside.
The polite poet stays aloof, disguising
or outwitting them (the rhymes), or trying to sneak
them by. But they're fanatical, blazing
with zeal and sooner or later they're back (rhymes
and biddies), pounding at your door and poems,
same as always.

Dialogo

«Se l'uomo è nella storia non è niente.
La storia è un *marché aux puces*, non un sistema».
«Provvidenza e sistema sono tutt'uno
e il Provvidente è l'uomo».
«Dunque è provvidenziale
anche la pestilenza».
«La peste è il negativo del positivo,
è l'uomo che trasuda il suo contrario».
«Sempre avvolto però nel suo sudario».
«Il sistema ternario
secerne il male e lo espelle,
mentre il binario se lo porta dietro».
«Ma il ternario lo mette sottovetro
e se vince lo adora».
                              «Vade retro,
Satana!».

Dialogue

"If man is in history, that's something.
History's a *marché aux puces,* not a system."
"Providence and system are one and the same,
and the Provident is man."
"Then even plague
is providential."
"Plague is the negation of the positive,
it's man who sweats out his opposite."
"But always wrapped in his shroud."
"The ternary system
isolates evil and expels it,
while the binary carries it with it."
"But the ternary puts it under glass
and when it conquers it, worships it."
                              "Get thee behind me! Git,
Satan!"

Fanfara

lo storicismo dialettico
materialista
autofago
progressivo
immanente
irreversibile
sempre dentro
mai fuori
mai fallibile
fatto da noi
non da estranei
propalatori
di fanfaluche credibili
solo da pazzi

la meraviglia sintetica
non idiolettica
né individuale
anzi universale
il digiuno
che nutre tutti
e nessuno

il salto quantitativo
macché qualitativo
l'empireo
la tomba
in casa senza bisogno
che di se stessi e nemmeno
perché c'è chi provvede
ed è il dispiegamento
d'una morale
senza puntelli eccetto

Fanfare

dialectical historicism
materialistic
autophagous
progressive
immanent
irreversible
always within
never without
infallible
made by us
not by foreign
purveyors
of taradiddle credible
only to crazies

the synthetic marvel
not idiolectic
nor individual
but universal
the fast
that nourishes all
and none

the quantitative leap
anything but qualitative
the empyrean
the tomb
at home without need
except of themselves and not even
because there's a provider
and it's the disclosure
of a morality
unbuttressed save for

l'intervento
eventuale
di un capo carismatico
finché dura
o di diàdochi
non meno provvidenziali

l'eternità tascabile
economica
controllata
da scienziati
responsabili e bene
controllati

la morte
del buon selvaggio
delle opinioni
delle incerte certezze
delle epifanie
delle carestie
dell'individuo non funzionale
del prete dello stregone
dell'intellettuale

il trionfo
nel sistema trinitario
dell'ex primate
su se stesso su tutto
ma senza il trucco
della crosta in ammollo
nella noosfera
e delle bubbole
che spacciano i papisti
modernisti o frontisti
popolari
gli impronti!

la guerra
quando sia progressista
perché invade

the eventual
intervention
of a boss charismatic
so long as he lasts
or of no less providential
epigonoi

pocket-sized eternity
economical
controlled
by scientists responsible and well
controlled

the death
of the noble savage
of opinions
of uncertain certainties
of epiphanies
of famines
of the nonfunctional individual
of the priest of the wizard
of the intellectual

the triumph
in the Trinitarian system
of the ex-primate
over himself over everything
but minus the fraud
of the softening crust
of the noosphere
and the whoppers
put out by modernist
or impudent popular
frontist
papists!

war
when it's progressive
because violent nonviolent
it invades

violenta non violenta
secondo accade
ma sia l'ultima

e lo è sempre
per sua costituzione

tu dimmi
disingaggiato amico
a tutto questo
hai da fare obiezioni?

as it happens
but may be the last
and is last always
by its very nature

tell me
my disengaged friend
do you have any objections
to all this?

Satura II

Lettera

Venezia 19..

Il vecchio colonnello di cavalleria
ti offriva negroni bacardi e roederer brut
con l'etichetta rossa. Disse il suo nome ma,
aggiunse, era superfluo ricordarlo.
Non si curò del tuo: del mio meno che meno.
Gli habitués dell'albergo erano tutti amici
anche senza conoscersi: ma soltanto agli sgoccioli
di settembre. Qualcuno ci abbracciava
scambiandoci per altri senza neppure scusarsi,
anzi congratulandosi per il felice errore.
Spuntavano dall'oscuro i grandi, i dimenticati,
la vedova di Respighi, le eredi di Toscanini,
un necroforo della Tetrazzini, un omonimo
di Malpighi, Ramerrez-Martinelli,
nube d'argento, e Tullio Carminati,
una gloria per qualche superstite iniziato.
(Su tutti il Potestà delle Chiavi, un illustre, persuaso
che noi fossimo i veri e i degni avant le déluge
che poi non venne o fu
poco più di un surplus dell'Acqua Alta).
Il vecchio cavaliere ripeteva da sempre
tra un bourbon e un martini che mai steeplechase
lo vide tra i battuti. E concludeva
sui reumatismi che gli stroncarono le ali.
Si viveva tra eguali, troppo diversi
per detestarsi, ma fin troppo simili
nell'arte del galleggio. L'invitto radoteur
è morto da qualche anno, forse prima di te.
Con lui s'è spento l'ultimo tuo corteggiatore.

Letter

Venice, 19..

The old cavalry colonel
would offer you Negroni, Bacardi, and Red Label
Roederer Brut. He told you his name but added
that there was no point in remembering it.
He didn't care about yours, even less about mine.
Nobody knew anyone, but the hotel's habitués
were all friends: though only at the tag end
of September. Someone mistook us for someone else
and embraced us without even an apology
and then congratulated himself on his lucky gaffe.
From obscurity the forgotten celebrities emerged,
Respighi's widow, Toscanini's heirs,
Tetrazzini's pallbearer, a namesake
of Malpighi, Ramerrez-Martinelli,
a silvery haze, and Tullio Carminati,
pride and joy of a few surviving initiates.
(Top dog was the Keeper of the Keys, a personage
convinced we were true and proper worthies
avant le déluge, which then never arrived or was
little more than a surplus of the Acqua Alta).
The old cavalier, between a bourbon
and a martini, told us again and again
that he'd never lost in the steeplechase. And he invariably
concluded with the rheumatism that had clipped his wings.
We lived among equals, too different
to detest each other, but too much alike
in the art of staying afloat. The unvanquished *radoteur*
died a few years back, maybe before you.
With him died the last of your gallants.
Now only tourist buses come to the hotel.

Ora all'albergo giungono solo le carovane.
Non più il maestro della liquirizia
al meconio. Più nulla in quello spurgo
di canale. E neppure l'orchestrina
che al mio ingresso dal ponte
mi regalava il pot-pourri dell'ospite
nascosto dietro il paravento: il conte
di Lussemburgo.

The master of licorice-with-meconium
comes no more. Nothing else arrives in that enema
called a canal. And not even the little orchestra
which regaled me as I entered from the bridge
with the potpourri of the Guest-
Concealed-Behind-the-Screen: *The Count
of Luxembourg.*

Realismo non magico

Che cos'è la realtà

il grattacielo o il formichiere
il Logo o lo sbadiglio
l'influenza febbrile
o la fabbrile o quella
del psicagogo

Che cosa resta incrostato
nel cavo della memoria

la cresima, la bocciatura,
il primo figlio (non ne ho),
le prime botte prese
o date,
il primo giorno (quale?),
le nozze, i funerali,
la prima multa, la prima
grossa impostura,
la sveglia da cinque lire
a suoneria
o l'altra col ghirigoro dell'usignolo,
la banda all'Acquasola,
la Pira (La) non accesa ma a bagnomaria
tra le dolci sorelle
dell'Istituto di Radiologia,
le visite e la morte della zia
di Pietrasanta

e tanta
e tanta e troppa roba, non so quale

Non-Magical Realism

What's reality

the skyscraper or the anteater
the Logos or the yawn
influenza fever
or influence of *faber*
or psychagogue

What's still left encrusted
in the cave of memory

confirmation, flunking my exams,
the first-born son (I've none),
the first hard knocks taken
or given,
the first day (which?),
the wedding, the funeral,
the first fine, the first
gross prevarication,
the five-lire wake-up
alarm-clock
or the other with the nightingale trill,
the band at the Acquasola,
the Pira (The) not lit but on bain-marie
among the sweet sisters
of the Institute of Radiology,
the visits and death of the aunt
from Pietrasanta

and so much
and so much and too much stuff, I don't know which

Che cosa di noi resta
agli altri
(nulla di nulla all'Altro)
quando avremo dimesso
noi stessi
e non penseremo ai pensieri
che abbiamo avuto perché
non lo permetterà
Chi potrà o non potrà,
questo non posso dirlo.

Ed è l'impaccio,
la sola obiezione che si fa
a chi vorrebbe abbattere il feticcio
dell'Inutilità.

What of us is left
to others
(nothing of nothing to the Other)
when we've laid
ourselves aside
and won't think of thoughts
we've had because
He won't permit it
the One who can or can't,
that I can't say.

And that's the problem,
the only objection we can make
to those who'd like to smash the Idol
of Uselessness.

Piove

Piove. È uno stillicidio
senza tonfi
di motorette o strilli
di bambini.

Piove
da un cielo che non ha
nuvole.
Piove
sul nulla che si fa
in queste ore di sciopero
generale.

Piove
sulla tua tomba
a San Felice
a Ema
e la terra non trema
perché non c'è terremoto
né guerra.

Piove
non sulla favola bella
di lontane stagioni,
ma sulla cartella
esattoriale,
piove sugli ossi di seppia
e sulla greppia nazionale.

Piove
sulla Gazzetta Ufficiale
qui dal balcone aperto,

It's Raining

It's raining. A drizzle
without backfiring
motorcycles or babies
crying.

It's raining
from a sky without
clouds.
It's raining
on the nothing we do
in these hours of general
strike.

It's raining
on your grave at San Felice
at Ema
and the earth isn't shaking
because there's no earthquake
or war.

It's raining
not on the lovely tale
of seasons past,
but on the tax-collector's
briefcase,
it's raining on cuttlefish bones
and bureaucrats.

It's raining
on the Official Bulletin
here from the open balcony,
it's raining on Parliament,
it's raining on Via Solferino,

piove sul Parlamento,
piove su via Solferino,
piove senza che il vento
smuova le carte.

Piove
in assenza di Ermione
se Dio vuole,
piove perché l'assenza
è universale
e se la terra non trema
è perché Arcetri a lei
non l'ha ordinato.

Piove sui nuovi epistèmi
del primate a due piedi,
sull'uomo indiato, sul cielo
ominizzato, sul ceffo
dei teologi in tuta
o paludati,
piove sul progresso
della contestazione,
piove sui works in regress,
piove
sui cipressi malati
del cimitero, sgocciola
sulla pubblica opinione.

Piove ma dove appari
non è acqua né atmosfera,
piove perché se non sei
è solo la mancanza
e può affogare.

it's raining without the wind's
ruffling the cards.

It's raining
in Hermione's absence
God willing,
it's raining because absence
is universal
and if the earth isn't quaking
it's because Arcetri
didn't command it.

It's raining on the new epistemes
of the biped primate,
on deified man, on the humanized
heavens, on the snouts
of theologians in overalls
or tuxedos,
it's raining on the progress
of the lawsuit,
it's raining
on work-in-regress,
on the ailing cypresses
in the cemetery, drizzling
on public opinion.

It's raining but if you appear
it's not water, not atmosphere,
it's raining because when you're not here,
it's nothing but absence
and absence can drown.

Gli ultimi spari

Moscerino, moschina erano nomi
non sempre pertinenti al tuo carattere
dolcemente tenace. Soccorrendoci
l'arte di Stanislaus poi decidemmo
per hellish fly. Volavi poco quando,
catafratta di calce, affumicata
da una stufa a petrolio eri la preda
di chi non venne e ritardò l'agguato.
E niente inferno
là dentro: solo tiri che da Fiesole
sfioravano il terrazzo, batteria
da concerto, non guerra. Fu la pace
quando scattasti, burattino mosso
da una molla, a cercare in un cestino
l'ultimo fico secco.

Parting Shots

"Moscerino" and "Moschina" were names
not always suited to your sweetly
willful disposition. Thanks to Stanislaus's
knack with names, we later settled on
(English) "Hell-fly." You didn't do much flying
when, caparisoned cap-a-pie in lime, and smoked
by a kerosene stove, you were the victim
of those who foiled your ambush by failing
to come. And there was nothing of hell
in that ambush: just a volley from Fiesole
that grazed the terrace: orchestral
barrage, not real war. Peace arrived
when you sprang up, a puppet triggered
by a spring, and went rummaging in a basket
for the last dry fig.

Le revenant

. . . .
quattro sillabe, il nome di un ignoto
da te mai più incontrato e senza dubbio morto.
Certamente un pittore; t'ha fatto anche la corte,
lo ammettevi, ma appena: era timido.
Se n'è parlato tra noi molti anni orsono; poi tu
non c'eri più e ne ho scordato il nome.
Ed ecco una rivista clandestina con volti
e pitture di artisti 'stroncati in boccio'
ai primi del 900. E c'è un suo quadro
orrendo, ma chi può dirlo? domani sarà un capodopera.
Sei stata forse la sua Clizia senza
saperlo. La notizia non mi rallegra.
Mi chiedo perché i fili di due rocchetti
si sono tanto imbrogliati; e se non sia quel fantasma
l'autentico smarrito e il suo facsimile io.

Le Revenant

. . . .

four syllables, the name of a stranger
never met again and doubtless dead.
A painter, for sure. He even courted you,
you admitted, but barely: he was shy.
We talked about it many years ago: then you
were no longer there and I forgot his name.
But here's an underground journal with faces
and drawings by artists "nipped in the bud"
in the first years of the century. And there's a hideous
painting by him. But who knows? By tomorrow it will be
a masterpiece. You may have been his Clizia
unknowingly. Not a happy thought for me.
I wonder how tapes from two reels
got so tangled together, and whether that ghost
could be the original and me the copy.

Niente di grave

Forse l'estate ha finito di vivere.
Si sono fatte rare anche le cicale.
Sentirne ancora una che scricchia è un tuffo nel sangue.
La crosta del mondo si chiude, com'era prevedibile
se prelude a uno scoppio. Era improbabile
anche l'uomo, si afferma. Per la consolazione
di non so chi, lassù alla lotteria
è stato estratto il numero che non usciva mai.

Ma non ci sarà scoppio. Basta il peggio
che è infinito per natura mentre
il meglio dura poco. La sibilla trimurtica
esorcizza la Moira insufflando
vita nei nati-morti. È morto solo
chi pensa alle cicale. Se non se n'è avveduto
il torto è suo.

Nothing Serious

Maybe summer has given up the ghost.
Even the cicadas have all but vanished. The sound
of one, still shrilling, makes the blood leap.
Predictably, the world's crust closes over, as it would
if explosion were imminent. Man too
they said was improbable. In the lottery
overhead a number was drawn that never
turned up before, for whose benefit I don't know.

But there'll be no explosion. Indefinite
by nature, the worst lasts, the best
is brief. The trimurtic Sybil
exorcises Moira, breathing life
into the stillborn. The only dead man is the man
thinking of cicadas. And it's his own fault
if he's unaware of the fact.

Tempo e tempi

Non c'è un unico tempo: ci sono molti nastri
che paralleli slittano
spesso in senso contrario e raramente
s'intersecano. È quando si palesa
la sola verità che, disvelata,
viene subito espunta da chi sorveglia
i congegni e gli scambi. E si ripiomba
poi nell'unico tempo. Ma in quell'attimo
solo i pochi viventi si sono riconosciuti
per dirsi addion, non arrivederci.

Time and Times

There's no unique time, rather many tapes
running parallel,
often contradictory, and rarely
intersecting. But then the sole truth
is disclosed and, once disclosed, immediately
erased by whoever runs the recorder
and spins the dials. And then we fall back
into unique time. But in that instant
only the few people still alive
have recognized each other in time to say,
not be-seeing-you, but good-bye.

Vedo un uccello fermo sulla grondaia,
può sembrare un piccione ma è più snello
e ha un po' di ciuffo o forse è il vento,
chi può saperlo, i vetri sono chiusi.
Se lo vedi anche tu, quando ti svegliano
i fuoribordo, questo è tutto quanto
ci è dato di sapere sulla felicità.
Ha un prezzo troppo alto, non fa per noi e chi l'ha
non sa che farsene.

I spy a bird perched in the gutter,
a pigeon maybe but not so plump,
with a tiny crest, but who knows,
with the windows closed, could be the wind.
If the speedboats wake you up, and you
spy him too, that happiness is all
we're given to know. It costs too much,
is not for us, and those so gifted
haven't a clue what to do with it.

La belle dame sans merci

Certo i gabbiani cantonali hanno atteso invano
le briciole di pane che io gettavo
sul tuo balcone perché tu sentissi
anche chiusa nel sonno le loro strida.

Oggi manchiamo all'appuntamento tutti e due
e il nostro breakfast gela tra cataste
per me di libri inutili e per te di reliquie
che non so: calendari, astucci, fiale e creme.

Stupefacente il tuo volto s'ostina ancora, stagliato
sui fondali di calce del mattino;
ma una vita senz'ali non lo raggiunge e il suo fuoco
soffocato è il bagliore dell'accendìno.

La Belle Dame Sans Merci

Clearly the canton's gulls have been waiting hungrily
for the crumbs of bread I once tossed
on your balcony so you could hear
their cries even in your heavy sleep.

Today we both miss the appointment
and our breakfast grows cold among piles
of useless books for me and relics of who knows what
for you: calendars, cases, lotions, bottles.

Amazingly, your face persists, embossed
on the morning's background of chalk; a life
without wings can't touch it, and its stifled fire
is the flare of my cigarette lighter.

Nell'attesa

È strano che tanto tempo sia passato
dall'annunzio del grande crac: seppure
quel tempo e quella notizia siano esistiti.
L'abbiamo letto nei libri: il fuoco non li risparmia
e anche di noi rimarrà un'eco poco attendibile.
Attendo qualche nuova di me che mi rassicuri.
Attendo che mi si dica ciò che nasconde il mio nome.
Attendo con la fiducia di non sapere
perché chi sa dimentica persino
di essere stato in vita.

Waiting

Strange that so much time has passed
since the announcement of the Big Bang—supposing
that so much time and such news ever existed.
We've read about it in books: fire doesn't spare them
and even our echo will be barely audible.
I wait for some change in myself to reassure me.
I wait to be told what my name conceals.
I wait with the confidence of not knowing
since he who knows forgets even the fact
of having been alive.

Botta e risposta II

I

«Il solipsismo non è il tuo forte, come si dice.
Se fosse vero saresti qui, insabbiato
in questa Capri nordica dove il rombo
dei motoscafi impedisce il sonno
fino dalla primalba. Sono passati i tempi
di Monte Verità, dei suoi nudisti,
dei kulturali jerofanti alquanto
ambivalenti o peggio. Eppure, inorridisci,
non so che sia, ma qui qualcosa regge».

(lettera da Ascona)

II

Diafana come un velo la foglia secca
che il formicone spinge sull'ammattonato
ospita viaggiatori che salgono e scendono in fretta.
Sto curvo su slabbrature e crepe del terreno
entomologo-ecologo di me stesso.
Il monte che tu rimpiangi l'ho salito
a piedi con la valigia fino a mezza strada.
Non prometteva nulla di buono, trovai alloggio
letto crauti e salsicce in riva al lago.
Vivevo allora in cerca di fandonie
da vendere. In quel caso un musicologo
ottuagenario sordo, famoso, ignoto a me
e agli indigeni, quasi irreperibile.
Lo stanai, tornai pieno di notizie,
sperai di essere accolto come un asso
della speleologia.

Thrust and Parry II

I

"Solipsism isn't your forte, as they say.
If it were, you'd be here, buried in sand
in this Nordic Capri where the roar
of speedboats makes dozing difficult
after dawn. The days of Mt. Verità
with its nudists and hierophants of Kultur,
no less ambivalent or worse,
are over. And yet, you shudder,
something here, I don't know what, persists."

(letter from Ascona)

II

Transparent as gossamer the dry leaf
nudged by the big ant across the pavement
shelters voyagers scurrying up and down.
I'm bent over the cracked and wrinkled ground
of my entomologico-ecological self.
That mountain you miss I climbed
on foot halfway to the top, suitcase in hand.
It promised me nothing worth the climb; at the lakeside
I found lodging, bed, sausages and kraut.
At the time my life was a quest for tall tales
to hawk. In particular, a deaf but famous
octogenerian musicologist, unknown to both me
and the natives, and almost impossible to trace.
I tracked him down and came back loaded with news
hoping to be welcomed
as a speleological whiz.

E ora tutto è cambiato, un formicaio
vale l'altro ma questo mi attira di più.
Un tempo, tu lo sai, dissi alla donna miope
che portava il mio nome e ancora lo porta dov'è:
noi siamo due prove,
due bozze scorrette che il Proto
non degnò d'uno sguardo. Fu anche un lapsus
madornale, suppongo, l'americana di Brünnen
di cui poi leggemmo il suicidio.
Vivente tra milioni d'incompiuti per lei
non c'era altra scelta. Diceva
che ognuno tenta a suo modo
di passare oltre: oltre che?
Ricordavo Porfirio: le anime dei saggi
possono sopravvivere. Quei pochi
pensano vedono amano senz'occhi
né corpo o forma alcuna. Fanno a meno
del tempo e dello spazio, immarcescibili
avari (questo il greco
non lo disse e non è il caso di leggerlo).
Tirchi così? Per noi non esisteva
scrigno di sicurezza per difendervi
l'ultimo candelotto rimasto acceso.
Se mai fosse il lucignolo prossimo all'estinzione
dopo non era che il buio.
Non per tutti, Porfirio, ma per i dàtteri
di mare che noi siamo, incapsulati
in uno scoglio. Ora neppure attendo
che mi liberi un colpo di martello.

. . . .

Se potessi vedermi tu diresti
che nulla è di roccioso in questo butterato
sabbiume di policromi
estivanti ed io in mezzo, più arlecchino
degli altri. Ma la sera poi sorviene
e riconcilia e chiude. Si sta meglio.
A tarda notte mi sfilo dal mignolo l'anello,
nel dito abbronzato resta un cerchiolino pallido.
Non credere che io porti la penitenza a un estremo

And now everything's changed; one anthill's
as good as another, but this one is more appealing.
Once, you know, I told my myopic wife
who bore my name, and bears it still, wherever
she is: Look, we're two drafts,
two uncorrected sketches which Number One
never thought worth a look. And that American girl
from Brünnen whose suicide we read about—
she, too, I suppose, was a huge oversight.
Living among millions of people, to her incomplete,
there was no other choice. She used to say
that everyone in his own way tries
to surpass, to transcend. Transcend what?
I kept recalling Porphyry: the souls of sages
can survive death. Those rare souls think,
see, love, all without eyes; without
body or form. They do without
time and space, incorruptible
misers (the Greek text didn't say this
and there's no chance of so construing it).
Cheapskate sages? For us
there was no defence, no windscreen
to shelter the last guttering candle end.
If the firefly was on the edge of extinction,
later there was only darkness.
Not for all, Porphyry, only for those poor
piddocks we are, shells
on a reef. Now I don't imagine
even a sledgehammer could set me free.

. . . .

If you could see me, you'd say
there was nothing rocklike in this pocked
sandpack of summering
polychromes with me in the middle, more of a clown
than others. But then evening comes on,
soothing, closing down. One feels better.
Late at night I slip the ring from my little finger,
leaving a small white circle on the tanned skin.
Don't suppose my remorse implies a potent

gusto di evanescenze e dilettazioni morose.
Nel buio e nella risacca più non m'immergo, resisto
ben vivo vicino alla proda, mi basto come mai prima
m'era accaduto. È questione
d'orgoglio e temperamento. Sto attento a tutto. Se occorre,
spire di zampironi tentano di salvarmi
dalle zanzare che pinzano, tanto più sveglie di me.

yen for transience and morbid delights.
I no longer dive into darkness and backwash.
I resist, very much alive, close to shore. I'm more
self-sufficient than before. A matter of pride
and temperament. I'm alert to everything. If needed,
I have insecticides, spirals of smoke, to stave off
the voracious mosquitoes, all livelier than me.

Qui e là

Da tempo stiamo provando la rappresentazione
ma il guaio è che non siamo sempre gli stessi.
Molti sono già morti, altri cambiano sesso,
mutano barbe volti lingua o età.
Da anni prepariamo (da secoli) le parti,
la tirata di fondo o solamente
'il signore è servito' e nulla più.
Da millenni attendiamo che qualcuno
ci saluti al proscenio con battimani
o anche con qualche fischio, non importa,
purché ci riconforti un *nous sommes là*.
Purtroppo non pensiamo in francese e così
restiamo sempre al qui e mai al là.

Here and There

For some time we've been rehearsing the show
but the problem is that we don't stay the same.
Many have died already, others change sex,
beards, faces, language, or age.
For years (centuries) we've been working on our parts,
the long, crucial tirade or merely
"Your humble servant, milord," and nothing more.
For millennia we've been waiting for someone
to hail us on the stage, with cheering
or even occasional boos, anything at all,
so long as there's a *nous sommes là* to console us.
Regrettably we don't think in French, which means
we're always here and never there.

Che mastice tiene insieme
questi quattro sassi.

Penso agli angeli
sparsi qua e là
inosservati
non pennuti non formati
neppure occhiuti
anzi ignari
della loro parvenza
e della nostra
anche se sono
un contrappeso più forte
del punto di Archimede
e se nessuno li vede
è perché occorrono altri occhi
che non ho
e non desidero.

La verità è sulla terra
e questa non può saperla
non può volerla
a patto di distruggersi.

Così bisogna fingere
che qualcosa sia qui
tra i piedi tra le mani
non atto né passato
né futuro
e meno ancora un muro
da varcare

What mortar bonds
these four stones.

I think of angels
scattered here and there
unobserved
without wings, without form
without even eyes
ignorant even
of their own appearance
and ours
and even if they're
a counterweight stronger
than Archimedes' point
and nobody sees them
it's because different eyes are needed
which I don't have
and don't want.

Truth is here on earth
and the earth can't know it
can't want it
except by destroying itself.

So we have to pretend
there's something here
between our feet between our hands
not about to be nor past
nor future
and still less a wall
to cross

bisogna fingere
che movimento e stasi
abbiano il senso
del nonsenso
per comprendere
che il punto fermo è un tutto
nientificato.

we have to pretend
that movement and stasis
have the sense
of nonsense
to understand
that the still point is a whole
nullified.

Provo rimorso per avere schiacciato
la zanzara sul muro, la formica
sul pavimento.
Provo rimorso ma eccomi in abito scuro
per il congresso, per il ricevimento.
Provo dolore per tutto, anche per l'ilota
che mi propina consigli di partecipazione,
dolore per il pezzente a cui non do l'elemosina,
dolore per il demente che presiede il consiglio
d'amministrazione.

I feel remorse for squashing the mosquito
on the wall, the ant
on the sidewalk.
I feel remorse, but here I am formally garbed
for the conference, the reception.
I feel sorry for all, even for the slave
who proffers me advice on the stock market,
sorrow for the beggar who gets no alms from me,
sorrow for the madman who presides
at the Administrative Council.

Auf Wiedersehen

hasta la vista, à bientôt, I'll be seeing you, appuntamenti
ridicoli perché si sa che chi s'è visto s'è visto.
La verità è che nulla si era veduto
e che un accadimento non è mai accaduto.
Ma senza questo inganno sarebbe inesplicabile
l'ardua speculazione che mira alle riforme
essendo il *ri* pleonastico là dove
manca la forma.

Auf Wiedersehen

hasta la vista, à bientôt, I'll be seeing you, absurd
arrangements, since we know the seeing's over, done with, *finito.*
The fact is that nothing was ever seen,
and that an occurrence never occurred.
But lacking this illusion the lofty speculation
that aims at reforms in which the *re-* is redundant
when the *-form* is missing, couldn't
be explained.

Cielo e terra

Che il cielo scenda in terra da qualche secolo
sempre più veloce
non lo potevi credere. Ora che mi è impossibile
dirtelo a voce ti svelo che non è sceso mai
perché il cielo non è un boomerang
gettato per vederselo ritornare.
Se l'abbiamo creato non si fa rivedere,
privo del connotato dell'esistenza.
Ma se così non è può fare senza
di noi, sue scorie, e della nostra storia.

Heaven and Earth

You couldn't believe that for centuries now
heaven has been descending to earth
ever more rapidly. Now that I can no longer tell you
myself, I'll show you it never did descend:
Heaven's not a boomerang we can throw
in order to see it returning.
If we created it, it can't be seen again
without the connotation of existence.
But if that's how things are, it can do
without us, its refuse, and our history.

Un mese tra i bambini

I bambini giocano
nuovissimi giuochi,
noiose astruse propaggini
del giuoco dell'Oca.

I bambini tengono in mano
il nostro avvenire.
Non questi che lo palleggiano,
ma generazioni lontane.

Il fatto non ha importanza
e gli ascendenti neppure.
Quello che hanno tra i piedi
è il presente e ne avanza.

I bambini non hanno
amor di Dio e opinioni.
Se scoprono la finocchiona
sputano pappe e emulsioni.

I bambini sono teneri
e feroci. Non sanno
la differenza che c'è
tra un corpo e la sua cenere.

I bambini non amano
la natura ma la prendono.
Tra i pini innalzano tende,
sciamano come pecchie.

A Month among Children

Children play
the latest games,
boring abstract variants
on the game of Goose.

Children hold our future
in their hands.
Not these children playing ball,
but future generations.

Facts don't matter
nor forebears either.
What lies between their feet
is the present, abounding.

Children have no love
for God and opinions.
If they discover salami,
they spurn pap and pablum.

Children are tender
and cruel. They don't know
the difference between
a body and its ashes.

Children have no love
for nature but they make it theirs,
pitching tents in the pines,
swarming like bees.

I bambini non pungono
ma fracassano. Spuntano
come folletti, s'infilano
negl'interstizi più stretti.

I bambini sopportano
solo le vecchie e i vecchi.
Arrampicativisi strappano
fermagli pendagli cernecchi.

I bambini sono felici
come mai prima. Con nomi
da rotocalco appaiono
nella réclame delle lavatrici.

I bambini non si chiedono
se esista un'altra Esistenza.
E hanno ragione. Quel nòcciolo
duro non è semenza.

I bambini . . .

Children don't sting,
they smash. They sprout
like elves, slithering
through the tiniest chinks.

Children can't stand anyone
but old men and women,
clambering up, grabbing
at curls, pins, and pendants.

Children are happy
as never before. They appear
in glossy magazines
advertising washing machines.

Children don't ask themselves
if there's another Existence.
And they're right. That hard nut
isn't a seed.

Children . . .

A pianterreno

Scoprimmo che al porcospino
piaceva la pasta al ragù.
Veniva a notte alta, lasciavamo
il piatto a terra in cucina.
Teneva i figli infruscati
vicino al muro del garage.
Erano molto piccoli, gomitoli.
Che fossero poi tanti
il guardia, sempre alticcio, non n'era sicuro.
Più tardi il riccio fu visto
nell'orto dei carabinieri.
Non c'eravamo accorti
di un buco tra i rampicanti.

On the Ground Floor

We discovered the porcupine
had a yen for pasta *al ragù*.
She came in late, we'd leave
the plate on the kitchen floor.
She kept her cubs all curled up
near the wall of the garage—
little balls of yarn, so small
the caretaker, always plastered,
wasn't sure of the size of the litter.
Later the porky was spotted
in the carabinieri's garden.
We hadn't spied the crawlway
cutting through the creepers.

A tarda notte

Il colloquio con le ombre
non si fa per telefono.
Sui nostri dialoghi muti non s'affaccia
'giraffa' o altoparlante.
Anche le parole però servono
quando non ci riguardano,
captate per errore di una centralinista
e rivolte a qualcuno
che non c'è,
che non sente.
Vennero da Vancouver una volta
a tarda notte
e attendevo Milano. Fui sorpreso
dapprima, poi sperai che continuasse
l'equivoco. Una voce dal Pacifico,
l'altra dalla laguna. E quella volta
parlarono due voci libere come non mai.
Poi non accadde nulla, assicurammo
l'intrusa del servizio che tutto era perfetto,
regolare e poteva continuare,
anzi *doveva*. Né sapemmo mai
su quali spalle poi gravasse il prezzo
di quel miracolo.
Ma non ne ricordai una parola.
Il fuso orario era diverso, l'altra
voce non c'era, non c'ero io per lei,
anche le lingue erano miste, un'olla
podrida di più gerghi, di bestemmie e di risa.
Ormai dopo tanti anni l'altra voce
non lo rammenta e forse mi crede morto.
Io credo che lo sia lei. Fu viva almeno un attimo
e non se n'è mai accorta.

Late at Night

There's no conversing with shades
on the telephone.
No loudspeaker or mike boom
appears in our mute dialogues.
Still, words are useful
when we're not involved, when they're
picked up accidentally by some operator
and relayed to someone else
who isn't there,
who doesn't hear.
Once, late at night, they came
from Vancouver, when I was expecting
a call from Milan.
I was surprised at first, then hoped
the confusion would continue: one voice
from the Pacific, another from the Venetian lagoon.
And on that occasion the two voices spoke
more freely than ever before.
Then total silence, and when the operator
broke in, we assured her that everything
was perfectly in order and the conversation could,
and *should,* continue. And we had no idea
who in the end would have to foot the bill
for that miracle.
But I don't remember a word of it.
The time zones were different, the other voice
wasn't there for me, and I wasn't here for her;
even the languages got jumbled, an olla
podrida of garbled slang, curses, and laughter.
By now, after so many years, the other voice
has forgotten, maybe she thinks I'm dead.
I think it's she who died. For at least a second
she was alive,
unawares.

Incespicare

Incespicare, incepparsi
è necessario
per destare la lingua
dal suo torpore.
Ma la balbuzie non basta
e se anche fa meno rumore
è guasta lei pure. Così
bisogna rassegnarsi
a un mezzo parlare. Una volta
qualcuno parlò per intero
e fu incomprensibile. Certo
credeva di essere l'ultimo
parlante. Invece è accaduto
che tutti ancora parlano
e il mondo
da allora è muto.

Stuttering

Stuttering, stammering,
need must be
to rouse the language
from its torpor.
But lisping won't do,
and although less noisy,
it's ruinous too. So
we'll have to be resigned
to half-speech. Once
somebody's speech was whole,
incomprehensibly so. Clearly
he believed he was the last
speaker. Instead, it fell out
that everyone's still talking
and ever since
the world's been mute.

Botta e risposta III

I

«Ho riveduto il tetro dormitorio
dove ti rifugiasti quando l'Almanacco
di Gotha straripò dalle soffitte
del King George e fu impietoso al povero
malnato. Già la pentola bolliva
e a stento bolle ancora mentre scrivo.
Mi resta il clavicembalo arrivato
nuovo di zecca. Ha un suono dolce e quasi
attutisce (per poco) il borbottìo
di quel bollore. Meglio non rispondermi».

(lettera da Kifissia)

II

Di quel mio primo rifugio
io non ricordo che le ombre
degli eucalipti; ma le altre,
le ombre che si nascondono
tra le parole, imprendibili,
mai palesate, mai scritte,
mai dette per intero,
le sole che non temono
contravvenzioni,
persecuzioni, manette,
non hanno né un prima né un dopo
perché sono l'essenza della memoria.
Hanno una forma di sopravvivenza
che non interessa la storia,

Thrust and Parry III

I

"I went back to see the dreary flophouse
where you took refuge when the *Almanach
de Gotha* overflowed from the attics
of the King George Hotel and had no pity
for the poor wretch. The pot was already boiling
and is still simmering now as I write.
I still have the harpsichord which arrived
spanking new. The tone is lovely and (for
a while) it almost drowns out the mutter
of that boiling pot. Best not reply."

(letter from Kifissia)

II

All I remember of that first refuge
of mine are the shadows
of the eucalyptus, but the others,
the shadows concealed
between words, unseizable,
never revealed, never written,
never wholly uttered,
the only ones that have no fear
of breaking the law,
persecutions, handcuffs.
Being the essence of memory,
they have neither before nor after.
They have a form of survival
of no importance to history,

una presenza scaltra, un'asfissia che non è
solo dolore e penitenza.

E posso dirti senza orgoglio,
ma è inutile perché
in questo mi rassomigli,
che c'è tra il martire e il coniglio,
tra la galera e l'esilio,
un luogo dove l'inerme
lubrifica le sue armi,
poche ma durature.

Resistere al vincitore
merita plausi e coccarde,
resistere ai vinti quand'essi
si destano e sono i peggiori,
resistere al peggio che simula
il meglio vuol dire essere salvi
dall'infamia, scampati (ma è un inganno)
dal solo habitat respirabile
da chi pretende che esistere
sia veramente possibile.

Ricordo ancora l'ostiere
di Xilocastron, il menu
dove lessi barbunia, indovinai
ch'erano triglie e lo furono,
anche se marce, e mi parvero
un dono degli dèi. Tutto ricordo
del tuo paese, del suo mare, delle
sue capre, dei suoi uomini,
eredi inattendibili di un mondo
che s'impara sui libri ed era forse
orrendo come il nostro.
Io ero un nume
in abito turistico, qualcosa
come il Viandante della Tetralogia,
ma disarmato, innocuo, dissotterrato,
esportabile
di contrabbando da uno specialista.

a shrewd presence, a suffocation which is not
merely penitence and pain.

And I can tell you this without pride,
but it's useless
since in this you resemble me,
and between the martyr and the rabbit,
between prison and exile,
there's a place where the defenceless man

oils his weapons,
few but permanent.
To resist the victor
deserves applause and ribbons,
resisting the defeated when they
waken and are the worst,
resisting the worst that simulates the best
means being safe
from infamy, liberated (but it's
an illusion) from the one habitat
in which those who pretend
existence is really possible
can breathe.

I still remember the inn
at Xilocastron, the menu
listing "Barbunia," which I guessed
were mullet, and they were,
even though spoiled, and to me they seemed
a gift from heaven. I remember everything
about your village, your sea, your
goats, your men,
unreliable heirs of a world
that knows itself from books and was perhaps
as awful as our own.
I was a divinity
in tourist garb, something
like the Wayfarer in the Tetralogy,
but unarmed, innocuous, disinterred,

Ma ero pur sempre nel divino. Ora
vivo dentro due chiese che si spappolano,
dissacrate da sempre, mercuriali,
dove i pesci che a gara vi boccheggiano
sono del tutto eguali. Se non fosse
che la pietà è inesauribile eppure
è un intralcio di più, direi che è usata male.
Ma la merito anch'io? Lascio irrisolto
il problema, sigillo questa lettera
e la metto da parte. La ventura
e la censura hanno in comune solo
la rima. E non è molto.

someone to be smuggled out
by a specialist.

But the divine was always with me. Now
I live between two overripe churches,
forever deconsecrated, marketplaces
where competitively gasping fish
are all the same. Except for the fact
that mercy is inexhaustible and yet it's
one more obstacle, misused I'd say.
But do I deserve it too? I leave the problem
unresolved, seal this letter
and set it aside. Venture
and censure have nothing in common
but the rhyme. Which isn't much.

È ridicolo credere

che gli uomini di domani
possano essere uomini,
ridicolo pensare
che la scimmia sperasse
di camminare un giorno
su due zampe

è ridicolo
ipotecare il tempo
e lo è altrettanto
immaginare un tempo
suddiviso in più tempi

e più che mai
supporre che qualcosa
esista
fuori dell'esistibile,
il solo che si guarda
dall'esistere.

It's Absurd Believing

that the men of tomorrow
can be men,
absurd to think
the ape hoped
someday to walk
on two feet

absurd
to mortgage time
and just as absurd
to imagine a time
subdivided into more times

and still more so
to suppose that anything
exists
outside the existible,
the uniqueness that desists
from existing.

Le parole

Le parole
se si ridestano
rifiutano la sede
più propizia, la carta
di Fabriano, l'inchiostro
di china, la cartella
di cuoio o di velluto
che le tenga in segreto;

le parole
quando si svegliano
si adagiano sul retro
delle fatture, sui margini
dei bollettini del lotto,
sulle partecipazioni
matrimoniali o di lutto;

le parole
non chiedono di meglio
che l'imbroglio dei tasti
nell'Olivetti portatile,
che il buio dei taschini
del panciotto, che il fondo
del cestino, ridottevi
in pallottole;

le parole
non sono affatto felici
di esser buttate fuori
come zambracche e accolte
con furore di plausi
e disonore;

Words

Words
when wakened
reject the most propitious
setting, the Fabriano
bond, the China
ink, the binding
leather or velvet
that sets them apart;

words
when they wake
lounge on the back
of bills, on the edges
of lottery tickets,
on wedding or funeral
invitations;

words
ask nothing more
than the clatter of the keys
on the Olivetti portable,
the darkness of jacket
pockets, the bottom
of the wastebasket, crumpled
into little balls;

words
aren't the least bit happy
at being tossed out
like whores and greeted
with cheers of applause
and disgrace;

le parole
preferiscono il sonno
nella bottiglia al ludibrio
di essere lette, vendute,
imbalsamate, ibernate;

le parole
sono di tutti e invano
si celano nei dizionari
perché c'è sempre il marrano
che dissotterra i tartufi
più puzzolenti e più rari;

le parole
dopo un'eterna attesa
rinunziano alla speranza
di essere pronunziate
una volta per tutte
e poi morire
con chi le ha possedute.

words
would prefer to sleep
in a bottle than the ignominy
of being read, sold, embalmed,
forced to hibernate;

words
belong to everyone and vainly
take cover in dictionaries
since there's always some boor
who roots up the rarest
and rankest truffles;

words
after waiting an eternity
renounce the hope
of being pronounced
once and for all
and then dying
with their possessor.

Fine del '68

Ho contemplato dalla luna, o quasi,
il modesto pianeta che contiene
filosofia, teologia, politica,
pornografia, letteratura, scienze
palesi o arcane. Dentro c'è anche l'uomo,
ed io tra questi. E tutto è molto strano.

Tra poche ore sarà notte e l'anno
finirà tra esplosioni di spumanti
e di petardi. Forse di bombe o peggio,
ma non qui dove sto. Se uno muore
non importa a nessuno purché sia
sconosciuto e lontano.

Year's End: 1968

From the moon, or thereabouts,
I've studied this modest planet which contains
philosophy, theology, politics,
pornography, literature, science,
hard or occult. It also contains man,
myself included. And it's all very strange.

In a few more hours it will be night,
and the year will end with exploding champagne
and firecrackers. Maybe bombs, or worse,
but not here where I am. If someone dies,
who cares, so long as he's unknown
and from elsewhere.

Divinità in incognito

Dicono
che di terrestri divinità tra noi
se ne incontrano sempre meno.
Molte persone dubitano
della loro esistenza su questa terra.
Dicono
che in questo mondo o sopra ce n'è una sola o nessuna;
credono
che i savi antichi fossero tutti pazzi,
schiavi di sortilegi se opinavano
che qualche nume in incognito
li visitasse.

Io dico
che immortali invisibili
agli altri e forse inconsci
del loro privilegio,
deità in fustagno e tascapane,
sacerdotesse in gabardine e sandali,
pizie assorte nel fumo di un gran falò di pigne,
numinose fantasime non irreali, tangibili,
toccate mai,
io ne ho vedute più volte
ma era troppo tardi se tentavo
di smascherarle.

Dicono
che gli dèi non discendono quaggiù,
che il creatore non cala col paracadute,
che il fondatore non fonda perché nessuno
l'ha mai fondato o fonduto
e noi siamo solo disguidi
del suo nullificante magistero;

Divinity in Disguise

They say
encounters between the terrestrial gods
and us happen less and less often.
Many people doubt
that gods exist on this earth.
They say
that in this world or the world above there's only
one god or none; they think
the ancient sages were all crazy,
slaves of divination, if they thought
they were visited by divinities
incognito.

I say
that immortals invisible
to others and maybe unaware
of being privileged,
gods in bluejeans and backpacks,
priestesses in raincoats and sandals,
Pythian sybils swathed in the smoke of a great bonfire
of pine cones, numinous phantoms, not unreal, tangible
but untouched—
I've glimpsed them now and then
but I wasn't fast enough
to unmask them.

They say
the gods no longer come down to earth,
that the creator doesn't come parachuting down,
that the founder doesn't found because no one
has ever founded or fondue'd him
and we're nothing but mistakes
of his nullifying power;

eppure
se una divinità, anche d'infimo grado,
mi ha sfiorato
quel brivido m'ha detto tutto e intanto
l'agnizione mancava e il non essente
essere dileguava.

and yet
if a god, even of the lowest rank,
has grazed me
that shiver told me all, and yet
there was no recognition, and the nonbeing
being faded away.

L'angelo nero

O grande angelo nero
fuligginoso riparami
sotto le tue ali,
che io possa sorradere
i pettini dei pruni, le luminarie dei forni
e inginocchiarmi
sui tizzi spenti se mai
vi resti qualche frangia
delle tue penne

o piccolo angelo buio,
non celestiale né umano,
angelo che traspari
trascolorante difforme
e multiforme, eguale
e ineguale nel rapido lampeggio
della tua incomprensibile fabulazione

o angelo nero disvélati
ma non uccidermi col tuo fulgore,
non dissipare la nebbia che ti aureola,
stàmpati nel mio pensiero
perché non c'è occhio che resista ai fari,
angelo di carbone che ti ripari
dentro lo scialle della caldarrostaia

grande angelo d'ebano
angelo fosco
o bianco, stanco di errare
se ti prendessi un'ala e la sentissi
scricchiolare
non potrei riconoscerti come faccio
nel sonno, nella veglia, nel mattino

The Black Angel

O great soot-black
angel, shelter me
under your wings,
let me scrape past
the bramble spikes, the oven's shining jets,
and fall to my knees
on the dead embers if perchance
some fringe of your feathers
remains

o small dark angel,
neither heavenly nor human,
angel who shines through,
changing colors, formless
and multiform, equal
and unequal in the swift lightning
of your incomprehensible fabulation

o black angel reveal yourself
but may your splendor not consume me,
leave unmelted the mist that haloes you,
stamp yourself in my thought,
since no eye resists your blazings
coal-black angel sheltering
under the chestnut peddler's cape

great ebony angel
angel dusky
or white
if, weary of my wandering,
I clutched your wing and felt it
crunch
I could not know you as now I do,

perché tra il vero e il falso non una cruna
può trattenere il bipede o il cammello,
e il bruciaticcio, il grumo
che resta sui polpastrelli
è meno dello spolvero
dell'ultima tua piuma, grande angelo
di cenere e di fumo, miniangelo
spazzacamino.

in sleep, on waking, in the morning
since between true and false no needle
can stop biped or camel,
and the charred residue, the grime
left on the fingertips
is less than the dust
of your last feather, great angel
of ash and smoke, mini-angel
chimney sweep.

L'Eufrate

Ho visto in sogno l'Eufrate,
il suo decorso sonnolento tra
tonfi di roditori e larghi indugi in sacche
di fango orlate di ragnateli arborei.
Chissà che cosa avrai visto tu in trent'anni
(magari cento) ammesso che sia qualcosa di te.
Non ripetermi che anche uno stuzzicadenti,
anche una briciola o un niente può contenere il tutto.
È quello che pensavo quando esisteva il mondo
ma il mio pensiero svaria, si appiccica dove può
per dirsi che non s'è spento. Lui stesso non ne sa nulla,
le vie che segue sono tante e a volte
per darsi ancora un nome si cerca sull'atlante.

The Euphrates

I saw the Euphrates in a dream,
its slow, sleepy progress among rodents
plopping, and its wide lingering in muddy
pockets fringed by spiderwebbing trees.
Who knows what you'll have seen in thirty years
(or even a hundred), though what you see is mostly you.
Don't tell me once more that a mere toothpick,
a crumb, a nothing, can contain the all.
That's what I thought when the world was still there,
but my thought forks and twists, clings where it can
simply to let itself know it hasn't
stopped. The river knows nothing of itself,
changing courses so often that, sometimes,
just to get a name, it consults the atlas.

L'Arno a Rovezzano

I grandi fiumi sono l'immagine del tempo,
crudele e impersonale. Osservati da un ponte
dichiarano la loro nullità inesorabile.
Solo l'ansa esitante di qualche paludoso
giuncheto, qualche specchio
che riluca tra folte sterpaglie e borraccina
può svelare che l'acqua come noi pensa se stessa
prima di farsi vortice e rapina.
Tanto tempo è passato, nulla è scorso
da quando ti cantavo al telefono 'tu
che fai l'addormentata' col triplice cachinno.
La tua casa era un lampo visto dal treno. Curva
sull'Arno come l'albero di Giuda
che voleva proteggerla. Forse c'è ancora o
non è che una rovina. Tutta piena,
mi dicevi, di insetti, inabitabile.
Altro comfort fa per noi ora, altro
sconforto.

The Arno at Rovezzano

Great rivers are the image of time,
impersonal and cruel. Viewed from a bridge,
they declare their inexorable nothingness.
Only the hesitant curve of some marshy
canebrake, a few shining pools
among dense scrub and mosses
can reveal that water, like us, reflects on itself
before turning into rapids and rapine.
So much time has passed, nothing's changed
since those days when, chortling like mad,
I sang you *"Toi qui fais l'endormie"* on the phone.
Seen from the train your house was a flash of light.
It leans over the Arno like the Judas tree
that tried to protect it. Maybe the house is still there,
maybe it's a shambles. Crawling with insects,
you told me, uninhabitable.
A different comfort suits us now, a different
discomfort.

Si andava . . .

Si andava per funghi
sui tappeti di muschio
dei castagni.

Si andava per grilli
e le lucciole
erano i nostri fanali.

Si andava per lucertole
e non ne ho mai
ucciso una.

Si andava sulle formiche
e ho sempre evitato
di pestarle.

Si andava all'abbecedario,
all'imbottimento primario,
secon-terziario, mortuario.

Si andava su male piste
e mai ne sono stato
collezionista.

Si andava per la gavetta,
per l'occupazione,
per la disdetta, per la vigilanza,
per la mala ventura.

Si andava non più per funghi
ma per i tempi lunghi
di un'età più sicura,
anzi per nessun tempo
perché non c'era toppa
nella serratura.

We Went . . .

We went for mushrooms
over the mossy carpets
under the chestnuts.

We went for crickets
and fireflies
lighted our way.

We went for lizards
and I never
killed one.

We went walking over ants
and I managed not
to squash any.

We went on to our ABCs,
to the crammings, primary,
secondo-tertiary, mortuary.

We went bad ways
and I never
collected any.

We went for the messkit,
the occupation,
repudiation, watchful waiting,
the dreadful outcome.

We no longer went for mushrooms,
we went for the tedious times
of a securer age,
or rather for no time at all,
trapped, up shit creek
without a paddle.

Annaspando

Si arraffa un qualche niente
e si ripete
che il tangibile è quanto basta.
Basterebbe un tangente
se non fosse
ch'è lì, a due passi, guasto.

Groping

You grab a few nothings
and remind yourself
that the tangible is all that counts.
Just a touch of something would do,
except that it's there, beside you,
busted.

Pasqua senza week-end

Se zufolo il segnale convenuto
sulle parole 'sabato domenica
e lunedì' dove potrò trovarti
nel vuoto universale? Fu un errore conoscersi,
un errore che tento di ripetere
perché solo il farnetico è certezza.

Easter without Weekend

If I whistle our signal—we agreed
on the words, "Saturday, Sunday,
Monday,"—where will I find you
in the universal void? We met by mistake,
a mistake I'm bent on repeating,
since only madness knows for sure.

Gli uomini che si voltano

Probabilmente
non sei più chi sei stata
ed è giusto che così sia.
Ha raschiato a dovere la carta a vetro
e su noi ogni linea si assottiglia.
Pure qualcosa fu scritto
sui fogli della nostra vita.
Metterli controluce è ingigantire quel segno,
formare un geroglifico più grande del diadema
che ti abbagliava.
Non apparirai più dal portello
dell'aliscafo o da fondali d'alghe,
sommozzatrice di fangose rapide
per dare un senso al nulla. Scenderai
sulle scale automatiche dei templi di Mercurio
tra cadaveri in maschera,
tu la sola vivente,
e non ti chiederai
se fu inganno, fu scelta, fu comunicazione
e chi di noi fosse il centro
a cui si tira con l'arco dal baraccone.
Non me lo chiedo neanch'io. Sono colui
che ha veduto un istante e tanto basta
a chi cammina incolonnato come ora
avviene a noi se siamo ancora in vita
o era un inganno crederlo. Si slitta.

Men Who Turn Back

Probably
you're no longer what you once were
and rightly so.
The emery board has duly worn us down,
our rough edges are all rubbed smooth.
Still, something was written
on the pages of our life.
Hold them against the light and the sign
is magnified—a hieroglyph larger than the diadem
that dazzled you.
Never again will you appear from the hatch
of the hovercraft or the seaweed on the bottom,
skin diver of muddy rapids
giving meaning to nothingness. You'll descend
on the escalators of Mercury's shrines—
the one living soul
among cadavers in disguise,
never once asking yourself
whether it was illusion, choice, communication,
and which of us was the bull's-eye
targeted by archers at the fairground booth.
Even I don't ask myself. I'm a man
who's seen an instant and that's enough
for someone filing past as we do now
if we're still alive
or were deluded in thinking so.
We slide along.

Ex voto

Accade
che le affinità d'anima non giungano
ai gesti e alle parole ma rimangano
effuse come un magnetismo. È raro
ma accade.

Può darsi
che sia vera soltanto la lontananza,
vero l'oblio, vera la foglia secca
più del fresco germoglio. Tanto e altro
può darsi o dirsi.

Comprendo
la tua caparbia volontà di essere sempre assente
perché solo così si manifesta
la tua magia. Innumeri le astuzie
che intendo.

Insisto
nel ricercarti nel fuscello e mai
nell'albero spiegato, mai nel pieno, sempre
nel vuoto: in quello che anche al trapano
resiste.

Era o non era
la volontà dei numi che presidiano
il tuo lontano focolare, strani
multiformi multanimi animali domestici;
fors'era così come mi pareva
o non era.

Ignoro
se la mia inesistenza appaga il tuo destino,

Ex Voto

It happens
that spiritual affinities don't become
gestures and words but radiate
like a magnetic field. It's rare but
it happens.

Maybe
only distance, only oblivion,
are real, the dry leaf more real
than the green shoot. This much, and more,
may be, or may be said to be.

I understand
your obstinate will always to be absent
since only by being so is your magic
made manifest. Your countless wiles
I intuit.

I insist
on seeking you in the shoot, never
in the unfolded tree, never at the full, always
in the void: in whatever resists even
the drill.

It was or it wasn't
the will of the powers that preside
over your distant hearth, strange
multiform multispirited household pets;
maybe that was how it seemed to me,
maybe not.

I don't know
if my nonexistence compensates your fate,

se la tua colma il mio che ne trabocca,
se l'innocenza è una colpa oppure
si coglie sulla soglia dei tuoi lari. Di me,
di te tutto conosco, tutto
ignoro.

if your fate brims, overflowing mine,
if innocence is a fault or trait
acquired at the threshold of your native home.
Of me, of you, I know everything,
and nothing at all.

Sono venuto al mondo . . .

Sono venuto al mondo in una stagione calma.
Molte porte si aprivano che ora si sono chiuse.
L'Alma Mater dormiva. Chi ha deciso
di risvegliarla?

Eppure
non furono così orrendi gli uragani del poi
se ancora si poteva andare, tenersi per mano,
riconoscersi.

E se non era facile muoversi tra gli eroi
della guerra, del vizio, della jattura,
essi avevano un viso, ora non c'è neppure
il modo di evitare le trappole. Sono troppe.

Le infinite chiusure e aperture
possono avere un senso per chi è dalla parte
che sola conta, del burattinaio.
Ma quello non domanda la collaborazione
di chi ignora i suoi fini e la sua arte.

E chi è da quella parte? Se c'è, credo
che si annoi più di noi. Con altri occhi
ne vedremmo più d'uno passeggiare
tra noi con meno noia e più disgusto.

I Came into the World . . .

I came into the world in a quiet time.
Many doors were opened which now are closed.
Alma Mater was asleep. Who decided
to rouse her?

And yet
hurricanes weren't so dreadful in those days:
we could still go strolling, hand in hand,
still recognize each other.

And though it was hard moving among heroes
of war, or vice, or misfortune, at least
they had faces; now there's no way
of avoiding the traps. There're too many.

The countless bottlenecks and loopholes
may have a meaning for those who side
with the Puppeteer, the only side that matters.
But He wants no collaboration from those
who know nothing of their ends and art.

And who sides with Him? If any, I think
they're more bored than we. Different eyes
will see a few of them strolling amongst us,
less bored and more disgusted.

Prima del viaggio

Prima del viaggio si scrutano gli orari,
le coincidenze, le soste, le pernottazioni
e le prenotazioni (di camere con bagno
o doccia, a un letto o due o addirittura un *flat*);
si consultano
le guide Hachette e quelle dei musei,
si cambiano valute, si dividono
franchi da escudos, rubli da copechi;
prima del viaggio s'informa
qualche amico o parente, si controllano
valige e passaporti, si completa
il corredo, si acquista un supplemento
di lamette da barba, eventualmente
si dà un'occhiata al testamento, pura
scaramanzia perché i disastri aerei
in percentuale sono nulla;
                              prima
del viaggio si è tranquilli ma si sospetta che
il saggio non si muova e che il piacere
di ritornare costi uno sproposito.
E poi si parte e tutto è O.K. e tutto
è per il meglio e inutile.

. . . .

                    E ora che ne sarà
del *mio* viaggio?
Troppo accuratamente l'ho studiato
senza saperne nulla. Un imprevisto
è la sola speranza. Ma mi dicono
ch'è una stoltezza dirselo.

Before the Trip

Before the trip we pore over timetables,
connections, stopovers, overnight stays
and reservations (rooms with bath
or shower, one bed or two, even a suite);
we consult
the Guides Hachettes and museum catalogues,
change money, sort francs
from escudos, rubles from kopecks;
before setting out we inform
friends or relatives, check
suitcases and passports,
equipment, buy extra
razor blades, and finally
glance at our wills, pure
knocking-on-wood since the percentage
of plane crashes is nil;
                              before
the trip we're calm while suspecting
that the wise don't travel and the pleasure
of returning is bought at a price.
And then we leave and everything's O.K. and everything's
for the best and pointless.

. . . .

                    And now what about
my journey?
I've arranged it too carefully
without knowing anything about it. An unexpected event
is my only hope. But they say
that's asking for trouble.

Le stagioni

Il mio sogno non è nelle quattro stagioni.

Non nell'inverno
che spinge accanto a stanchi termosifoni
e spruzza di ghiaccioli i capelli già grigi,
e non nei falò accesi nelle periferie
dalle pandemie erranti, non nel fumo
d'averno che lambisce i cornicioni
e neppure nell'albero di Natale
che sopravvive, forse, solo nelle prigioni.

Il mio sogno non è nella primavera,
l'età di cui ci parlano antichi fabulari,
e non nelle ramaglie che stentano a metter piume,
non nel tinnulo strido della marmotta
quando s'affaccia dal suo buco
e neanche nello schiudersi delle osterie e dei crotti
nell'illusione che ormai più non piova
o pioverà forse altrove, chissà dove.

Il mio sogno non è nell'estate
nevrotica di falsi miraggi e lunazioni
di malaugurio, nel fantoccio nero
dello spaventapasseri e nel reticolato
del tramaglio squarciato dai delfini,
non nei barbagli afosi dei suoi mattini
e non nelle subacquee peregrinazioni
di chi affonda con sé e col suo passato.

Il mio sogno non è nell'autunno
fumicoso, avvinato, rinvenibile
solo nei calendari o nelle fiere
del Barbanera, non nelle sue nere

The Seasons

My dream is not in the four seasons.

Not in winter
that pulls up close to tired radiators
and sprays icicles on hair already gray,
not in bonfires in the outskirts lit
by homeless vagrants, not in the miasmal
smoke lapping cornices and eaves,
and not even in the Christmas tree
which survives, maybe, only in prisons.

My dream is not in spring,
the fabled age of which the ancients speak,
not in pruned branches struggling to sprout,
nor the shrill chitter of the woodchuck
nosing from his burrow;
and not even in the opening of taverns and bistros
in the illusion that now the rain will stop,
or maybe go rain somewhere else, who knows where.

My dream is not in summer
neurotic with mirages and ill-omened
lunar months, nor in the scarecrow's
black puppet, nor the meshes
of the dragnet shredded by dolphins,
not in the humid glare of its mornings
and not in the underwater wanderings
of the man who drowns with himself and his past.

My dream is not in autumn
misty and musty, an autumn to be found
only in calendars and farmers'
almanacs, not in its black-

fulminee sere, nelle processioni
vendemmiali o liturgiche, nel grido dei pavoni,
nel giro dei frantoi, nell'intasarsi
della larva e del ghiro.

Il mio sogno non sorge mai dal grembo
delle stagioni, ma nell'intemporaneo
che vive dove muoiono le ragioni
e Dio sa s'era tempo; o s'era inutile.

lightninged evenings, in harvest
or holy-day processions, in the screams
of peacocks, in the turning
of olive presses, in shutting out
larva and dormouse.

My dream never rises from the womb
of the seasons, but in the timeless moment
that lives where reasons die and God only knows
whether it was time; or whether useless.

Dopo una fuga

C'erano le betulle, folte, per nascondere
il sanatorio dove una malata
per troppo amore della vita, in bilico
tra il tutto e il nulla si annoiava.
Cantava un grillo perfettamente incluso
nella progettazione clinica
insieme col cucù da te già udito
in Indonesia a minore prezzo.
C'erano le betulle, un'infermiera svizzera,
tre o quattro mentecatti nel cortile,
sul tavolino un album di uccelli esotici,
il telefono e qualche cioccolatino.
E c'ero anch'io, naturalmente, e altri
seccatori per darti quel conforto
che tu potevi distribuirci a josa
solo che avessimo gli occhi. Io li avevo.

★　★　★

Il tuo passo non è sacerdotale,
non l'hai appreso all'estero, alla scuola
di Jacques-Dalcroze, più smorfia che rituale.
Venne dall'Oceania il tuo, con qualche
spina di pesce nel calcagno. Accorsero
i congiunti, i primari, i secondari
ignari che le prode corallifere
non sono le Focette ma la spuma
dell'aldilà, l'exit dall'aldiqua.
Tre spine nel tuo piede, non tre pinne
di squalo, commestibili. Poi venne
ad avvolgerti un sonno artificiale.
Di te qualche susurro in teleselezione
con un prefisso lungo e lagne di intermediari.

After a Flight

There were birches, thick, to hide
the sanitarium where a woman, sick
from excess love of life, poised between all
and nothingness, was dying of boredom.
A cricket, included in the clinic's
ideal therapeutic plan, was chirping away
in concert with the cuckoo you'd once heard
in Indonesia at less expense.
There were birches, a Swiss nurse,
three or four crazies in the courtyard,
a volume of exotic birds on the table,
the phone, and some chocolates.
And I was there of course, and some other
bores, to provide you with that comfort
and cheer you would have lavished on us
if only we had eyes. And I did.

★   ★   ★

Your gait isn't priestlike,
you didn't acquire it abroad, at the École
Jacques-Delcroze—more affected than ceremonial.
Yours came from Oceania, along with a few
fishbones stuck in your heel. Your relatives,
your physicians, the interns all come running,
unaware that coral reefs
aren't Le Focette but the foam
of the beyond, the exit from the here-and-now.
Three fishbones in your foot, not three
quite edible shark fins. Then
you were swathed in artificial sleep.
Later there were murmurs from you on the phone
with its endless area codes, and other callers complaining.
Nothing else on the line, not even

Dal filo nient'altro, neppure un lieve passo felpato
dalla moquette. Il sonno di un acquario.

★ ★ ★

Gli Amerindi se tu
strappata via da un vortice fossi giunta laggiù
nei gangli vegetali in cui essi s'intricano
sempre più per sfuggire l'uomo bianco,
quei celesti ti avrebbero inghirlandata
di percussivi omaggi anche se non possiedi
i lunghi occhi a fessura delle mongole.
Tanto tempo durò la loro fuga: certo
molte generazioni. La tua, breve,
ti ha salvata dal buio o dall'artiglio
che ti aveva in ostaggio. E ora il telefono
non è più necessario per udirti.

★ ★ ★

La mia strada è passata
tra i demoni e gli dèi, indistinguibili.
Era tutto uno scambio di maschere, di barbe,
un volapük, un guaranì, un pungente
charabia che nessuno poteva intendere.
Ora non domandarmi perché t'ho identificata,
con quale volto e quale suono entrasti
in una testa assordita da troppi clacson.
Qualche legame o cappio è giunto fino a me
e tu evidentemente non ne sai nulla.
La prima volta il tuo cervello pareva
in evaporazione e il mio non era migliore.
Hai buttato un bicchiere dalla finestra,
poi una scarpa e quasi anche te stessa
se io non fossi stato vigile lì accanto.
Ma tu non ne sai nulla: se fu sogno
laccio tagliola è inutile domandarselo.
Anche la tua strada sicuramente
scavalcava l'inferno ed era come
dare l'addio a un eliso inabitabile.

a soft scuffing of slippers on the floor.
An aquarium sleep.

*   *   *

If you'd been ravished by a whirlwind,
and landed down here in those vegetable ganglia
in which the Amerindians tangle themselves
ever more deeply to escape the white man,
those celestials would have wreathed you
with tom-tom homage though you lack
the long slant eyes of Mongolian women.
Their flight lasted a long, long time: certainly
many generations. Yours, though brief,
saved you from the darkness or the claw
that held you hostage. And now I don't need
the phone to hear your voice.

*   *   *

My road made its way
among demons and gods, indistinguishable.
It was all an exchange of masks, of beards,
a Volapük, a Guarani, a harsh
jabberwocky no one could understand.
Now don't ask me how I identified you,
with what face and what sound you entered
this head deafened by too many honking horns.
Some tie or loop of which you evidently
were unaware reached and touched me.
The first time your brain seemed
to volatilize, and mine was no better.
You tossed a glass from the window,
then a shoe and almost would have jumped yourself
if I hadn't been nearby, keeping watch.
But you know nothing of it: no use now
asking whether it was dream, snare, or trap.
Certainly your road also straddled
hell and it was like saying good-bye
to an uninhabitable Elysium.

Mentre ti penso si staccano
veloci i fogli del calendario. Brutto
stamani il tempo e anche più pestifero
il Tempo. Di te il meglio
esplose tra lentischi rovi rivi
gracidìo di ranocchi voli brevi
di trampolieri a me ignoti (i Cavalieri
d'Italia, figuriamoci!) e io dormivo
insonne tra le muffe dei libri e dei brogliacci.
Di me esplose anche il pessimo: la voglia
di risalire gli anni, di sconfiggere
il pièveloce Crono con mille astuzie.
Si dice ch'io non creda a nulla, se non ai miracoli.
Ignoro che cosa credi tu, se in te stessa oppure
lasci che altri ti vedano e ti creino.
Ma questo è più che umano, è il privilegio
di chi sostiene il mondo senza conoscerlo.

★ ★ ★

Quando si giunse al borgo del massacro nazista,
Sant'Anna, su cui gravita un picco abrupto,
ti vidi arrampicarti come un capriolo
fino alla cima accanto a un'esile polacca
e al ratto d'acqua, tua guida, il più stambecco di tutti.
Io fermo per cinque ore sulla piazza
enumerando i morti sulla stele, mettendomici
dentro ad honorem ridicolmente. A sera
ci trasportò a sobbalzi il fuoribordo
dentro la Burlamacca,
una chiusa di sterco su cui scarica
acqua bollente un pseudo oleificio.
Forse è l'avanspettacolo dell'inferno.
I Burlamacchi, i Caponsacchi . . . spettri
di eresie, di illeggibili poemi.
La poesia e la fogna, due problemi
mai disgiunti (ma non te ne parlai).

While I think of you the pages
of the calendar fall away fast. Nasty
weather this morning and Time itself
deadlier still. The best of you
exploded among mastics briars brooks
frogs croaking brief flights
of wading birds unknown to me (called, just
imagine, Italian Cavaliers!), and I was sleeping
sleepless in the mildew of books and ledgers.
The worst of me exploded too: the yearning
to retrace the years and defeat
fleet-footed Chronos with a thousand ruses.
They say I believe in nothing, only miracles.
What you believe I don't know: in yourself
or else as others see you and create you.
But this is superhuman, the prerogative
of those who unknowingly shoulder the world.

* * *

When we reached Sant'Anna, the small town
of the Nazi massacre, dominated by a sheer peak,
I saw you, like a mountain goat, scrambling up
to the summit at the side of a slim Polish girl,
with your guide, the water rat, the supreme ibex.
For five hours I stood there in the piazza,
counting the names of the dead on the monument, absurdly
inserting myself *ad honorem*. That evening
the speedboat carried us leapfrogging
into the Burlamacca,
a dam of dung with boiling water spouting
over it like a phoney gusher.
Maybe this is the preview of hell.
The Burlamacchi, Caponsacchi . . . spectres
of heresies, of unreadable poems.
Poetry and the sewer, two inseparable
problems (but of this I said nothing to you).

★ ★ ★

Tardivo ricettore di neologismi
nel primo dormiveglia ero in dubbio
tra Hovercraft e Hydrofoil,
sul nome del volatile su cui intendevo involarti
furtivamente; e intanto tu eri fuggita
con un buon topo d'acqua di me più pronto
e ahimè tanto più giovane. Girovagai lentamente
l'intera lunga giornata e riflettevo
che tra re Lear e Cordelia non corsero tali pensieri
e che crollava così ogni lontano raffronto.
Tornai col gruppo visitando tombe
di Lucumoni, covi di aristocratici
travestiti da ladri, qualche piranesiana
e carceraria strada della vecchia Livorno.
M'infiltrai nei cunicoli del ciarpame. Stupendo
il cielo ma quasi orrifico in quel ritorno.
Anche il rapporto con la tragedia se ne andava ora in fumo
perché, per soprammercato, non sono nemmeno tuo padre.

★ ★ ★

Non posso respirare se sei lontana.
Così scriveva Keats a Fanny Brawne
da lui tolta dall'ombra. È strano che il mio caso
si parva licet sia diverso. Posso
respirare assai meglio se ti allontani.
La vicinanza ci riporta eventi
da ricordare: ma non quali accaddero,
preveduti da noi come futuri
sali da fiuto, ove occorrecsse, o aceto
dei sette ladri (ora nessuno sviene
per quisquilie del genere, il cuore a pezzi o simili).
È l'ammasso dei fatti su cui avviene l'impatto
e, presente cadavere, l'impalcatura non regge.
Non tento di parlartene. So che se mi leggi
pensi che mi hai fornito il propellente
necessario e che il resto (purché *non sia* silenzio)
poco importa.

Slow at accepting neologisms
I couldn't tell in my early morning drowsing
whether the name of the flying object
in which I meant to take flight with you
in secret was Hovercraft or Hydrofoil; and meanwhile
you'd taken off with a handsome water rat,
livelier than me and, alas, a great deal younger.
All day long I wandered slowly about, musing
that Lear and Cordelia had no such thoughts as these,
and that even the most remote comparisons crumbled.
I returned with the group, after visiting
the tombs of Lucumos, dens of aristocrats
disguised as thieves, and prison streets
à la Piranesi, in old Livorno. I burrowed
my way through rabbit holes of trash. The sky
was stupendous but almost terrifying
on the way back. Even the link with tragedy
dissolved in smoke since, in any case,
I'm not even your father.

* * *

I can't breathe when you're not here.
So Keats wrote to Fanny Brawne, plucked
by him from oblivion. It's strange,
but my case is different, *si parva licet.*
I breathe rather better when you're not here.
Closeness brings back events
to remember: but not as they happened,
foreseen by us as future smelling salts,
for use as needed, or pungent herbal
restoratives (no one faints these days, not
for such trifles as broken hearts, or the like).
What makes the impact is the accumulation of facts
and, when there's a corpse, the scaffolding
collapses. I won't try telling you about it.
If you're reading me, I know you're thinking
you've provided me with the stimulus I needed,
and that everything else (providing *it's not* silence)
doesn't much matter.

Piròpo, per concludere

Meravigliose le tue braccia. Quando
morirò vieni ad abbracciarmi, ma
senza il pull over.

Piròpo, in Conclusion

Your arms, so wonderful!
When I die, come embrace me,
but take off your sweater first.

Due prose veneziane

I

Dalle finestre si vedevano dattilografe.
Sotto, il vicolo, tanfo di scampi fritti,
qualche zaffata di nausea dal canale.
Bell'affare a Venezia
affacciarsi su quel paesaggio e lei
venuta da lontano. Lei che amava solo
Gesualdo Bach e Mozart e io l'orrido
repertorio operistico con qualche preferenza
per il peggiore. Poi a complicare le cose
l'orologio che segna le cinque e sono le quattro,
l'uscita intempestiva, San Marco, il Florian deserto,
la riva degli Schiavoni, la trattoria Paganelli
raccomandata da qualche avaro pittore toscano,
due camere neppure comunicanti e il giorno
dopo vederti tirar dritta senza
degnare di un'occhiata il mio Ranzoni.
Mi domandavo chi fosse nell'astrazione,
io lei o tutti e due, ma seguendo un binario
non parallelo, anzi inverso. E dire che avevamo
inventato mirabili fantasmi sulle rampe
che portano dall'Oltrarno al grande piazzale.
Ma ora lì tra piccioni,
fotografi ambulanti sotto un caldo bestiale,
col peso del catalogo della biennale
mai consultato e non facile da sbarazzarsene.
Torniamo col battello scavalcando becchime,
comprando keepsakes cartoline e occhiali scuri sulle bancarelle.
Era, mi pare, il '34, troppo giovani o troppo strani
per una città che domanda turisti e amanti anziani.

Two Venetian Sequences

I

From the windows we could see typists.
Below, the alley with its reek of fried scampi,
the sickening stench from the canal.
A superspecial treat, the sight of that landscape,
especially for her who had come to Venice
from a great distance—she who loved only Gesualdo,
Bach, and Mozart, and me with my horrible
operatic repertory and my penchant for music
even worse. Then, to complicate matters,
the clock that showed five when it was only four,
and our rushing out: St. Mark's, Florian's deserted,
Riva degli Schiavoni, the Trattoria Paganelli,
recommended by some mingy Tuscan painter,
two rooms, not even adjoining, and then the next day
when I saw you keep right on walking
without deigning even a glance at my Ranzoni.
I wondered who was the more distrait—
I, she, or both of us, each following paths
less parallel than opposed. And talk about
the glorious fantasies we'd had on the ramp
leading from the Oltrarno to the great piazza!
But there we were, in beastly heat, among pigeons
and strolling photographers,
burdened by the Biennale catalogue we never inspected
and which we disposed of only with difficulty.
We took the vaporetto back, crunching birdseed, buying
souvenirs, postcards and dark glasses at the stalls on the way.
It was, I believe, 1934, and we were too young or too strange
for a city that demands tourists or old lovers.

II

Il Farfarella garrulo portiere ligio agli ordini
disse ch'era vietato disturbare
l'uomo delle corride e dei safari.
Lo supplico di tentare, sono un amico di Pound
(esageravo alquanto) e merito un trattamento
particolare. Chissà che . . . L'altro alza la cornetta,
parla ascolta straparla ed ecco che
l'orso Hemingway ha abboccato all'amo.
È ancora a letto, dal pelame bucano
solo gli occhi e gli eczemi.
Due o tre bottiglie vuote di Merlot,
avanguardia del grosso che verrà.
Giù al ristorante tutti sono a tavola.
Parliamo non di lui ma della nostra
Adrienne Monnier carissima, di rue de l'Odéon,
di Sylvia Beach, di Larbaud, dei ruggenti anni trenta
e dei raglianti cinquanta. Parigi Londra un porcaio,
New York stinking, pestifera. Niente cacce in palude,
niente anatre selvatiche, niente ragazze
e nemmeno l'idea di un libro simile.
Compiliamo un elenco di amici comuni dei quali
ignoro il nome. Tutto è rotten, marcio.
Quasi piangendo m'impone di non mandargli gente
della mia risma, peggio se intelligenti.
Poi s'alza, si ravvolge in un accappatoio
e mi mette alla porta con un abbraccio.
Visse ancora qualche anno e morendo due volte
ebbe il tempo di leggere le sue necrologie.

II

Farfarella, the gabby doorman, obeying orders,
said he wasn't allowed to disturb the man
who wrote about bullfights and safaris.
I implore him to try, I'm a friend of Pound
(a slight exaggeration) and deserve special
treatment. Maybe . . . He picks up the phone,
talks listens pleads and, lo, the great bear
Hemingway takes the hook.
He's still in bed, all that emerges
from his hairy face are eyes and eczema.
Two or three empty bottles of Merlot,
forerunners of the gallon to come.
Down in the restaurant we're all at table.
We don't talk about him but about our dear friend
dear Adrienne Monnier, the Rue de L'Odéon,
about Sylvia Beach, Larbaud, the roaring thirties
and the braying fifties. Paris, pigsty London,
New York, nauseating, deadly. No hunting in the marshes,
no wild ducks, no girls, and not
the faintest thought of a book on such topics.
We compile a list of mutual friends whose names
I don't know. The world's gone to rot,
decaying. Almost in tears, he asks me not to send him
people of my sort, especially if they're intelligent.
Then he gets up, wraps himself in a bathrobe,
hugs me, and shows me to the door.
He lived on a few more years, and, dying twice,
had the time to read his own obituaries.

Il repertorio

Il repertorio
della memoria è logoro: una valigia di cuoio
che ha portato etichette di tanti alberghi.
Ora vi resta ancora qualche lista
che non oso scollare. Ci penseranno i facchini,
i portieri di notte, i tassisti.

Il repertorio della tua memoria
me l'hai dato tu stessa prima di andartene.
C'erano molti nomi di paesi, le date
dei soggiorni e alla fine una pagina in bianco,
ma con righe a puntini . . . quasi per suggerire,
se mai fosse possibile, 'continua'.

Il repertorio
della nostra memoria non si può immaginarlo
tagliato in due da una lama. È un foglio solo con tracce
di timbri, di abrasioni e qualche macchia di sangue.
Non era un passaporto, neppure un benservito.
Servire, anche sperarlo, sarebbe ancora la vita.

The Archive

The archive
of memory is wearing thin: a leather suitcase
that once sported labels from scores of hotels.
Now nothing's left but a few stickers
I don't dare remove. Bellhops, night
doormen, cabbies will see to that.

The archive of your memory
you gave to me yourself before moving on.
It contained a long list of countries, dates
of visits, and, at the end, a blank page
with dotted lines . . . as though to suggest,
if that were possible, "To be continued."

The archive
of our memory halved by a knife
is unthinkable. It's just one page with traces
of stamps, erasures, a few spots of blood.
It wasn't a passport, not even a recommendation
for services rendered. To serve, even the hope
of serving, would mean living again.

Laggiù

La terra sarà sorvegliata
da piattaforme astrali

Più probabili o meno si faranno
laggiù i macelli

Spariranno profeti e profezie
se mai ne furono

Scomparsi l'io il tu il noi il voi
dall'uso

Dire nascita morte inizio fine
sarà tutt'uno

Dire ieri domani
un abuso

Sperare—flatus vocis non compreso
da nessuno

Il Creatore avrà poco da fare
se n'ebbe

I santi poi bisognerà cercarli
tra i cani

. . . .

Gli angeli resteranno inespungibili
refusi.

Down Below

Space stations will maintain surveillance
over the earth

Down below massacres will be
more or less likely

Prophets will disappear, prophecies too
if there ever were any

I you we will all become
obsolete words

Birth death beginning end will all
be the same word

Hope—a *flatus vocis* understood
by nobody

The Creator will have little to do
if he ever did

You'll have to look for saints
among the dogs

. . . .

Angels will remain printer's errors
that can't be corrected.

Senza salvacondotto

Mi chiedo se Hannah Kahn
poté scampare al forno crematorio.
È venuta a trovarmi qualche volta
nel sotterraneo dove vegetavo
e l'invitavo a cena in altre 'buche'
perché mi parlava di te.
Diceva di esserti amica ma dubitai fosse solo
una tua seccatrice e in effetti
non esibì mai lettere o credenziali.
Può darsi che ti abbia vista di straforo
con me, senza di me sulla Scarpuccia
o sulla costa San Giorgio, quella dell'idolo d'oro.
Non fu indiscreta, comprese. Poi non la vidi più.
Se fu presa dal gorgo difficilmente poté
salvarsi con il tuo per me infallibile
passe-partout.

Without Safe-Conduct

I wonder if Hannah Kahn
managed to escape the gas chamber.
She came to see me on several occasions
in the storage basement where I was vegetating
and because she talked to me about you
I invited her to dine in other holes-in-the-wall.
She claimed to be your friend, but I suspected
you found her a pest and in fact
she never showed me letters or credentials.
Maybe her meetings with you were clandestine,
with or without me, on the Scarpuccia
or the Costa San Giorgio, the place of the golden idol.
She wasn't indiscreet, she understood. Then she vanished.
If the abyss took her, she would have found it hard
to save herself with your—to me infallible—
passe-partout.

Il genio

Il genio purtroppo non parla
per bocca sua.

Il genio lascia qualche traccia di zampetta
come la lepre sulla neve.

La natura del genio è che se smette
di camminare ogni congegno è colto
da paralisi.

Allora il mondo è fermo nell'attesa
che qualche lepre corra su improbabili
nevate.

Fermo e veloce nel suo girotondo
non può leggere impronte
sfarinate da tempo,
indecifrabili.

Genius

Regrettably genius doesn't speak
through its own mouth.

Genius leaves a few traces of footprints
like a hare in the snow.

It's the nature of genius that, when it stops
moving, every mechanism is stricken
with paralysis.

Then the world stops, waiting
for a hare or two to run across improbable
snowfalls.

Firm and swift in its circling dance
it can't read prints
turned to powder by time,
indecipherable.

La diacronia

Non si comprende come dalla pianura
spunti alcunché.

Non si comprende perché dalla buona ventura
esca la mala.

Tutto era liscio lucente emulsionato
d'infinitudine

e ora c'è l'intrudente il bugno la scintilla
dall'incudine.

Bisognerà lavorare di spugna su quanto escresce,
schiacciare in tempo le pustole di ciò che non s'appiana.

È una meta lontana ma provarcisi
un debito.

Diachronics

We don't understand why nothing sprouts
from the plain.

We don't understand why good luck
produces misfortune.

Everything was smooth shining liquid suspension
of infinitude

and now there's the intrusive the beehive the spark
from the anvil.

We'll have to sponge away every excrescence,
hammer down the pustules of what won't flatten.

It's a long-range goal but we're obliged
to give it a try.

Suoni

Tutta la vita è una musica
di sincopi.
Non più il filo che tiene,
non l'uggia
del capo e della coda, ma la raspa
e la grattugia.
Così da sempre; ma dapprima fu
raro chi se n'avvide. Solo ora l'ecumene
ama ciò che la uccide.

Sounds

All life is a syncopated
music.
No longer the continuous line,
nor the boredom
of *capo* and *coda*, but the rasp
and the grater.
It was always so, but seldom noticed
at first. Only now does the *ecumene*
love what kills it.

Il notaro

Il notaro ha biffato le lastre
dei miei originali.
Tutte meno una, me stesso,
già biffato all'origine
e non da lui.

The Notary

The notary X'd out the bloopers
in my original drafts.
All but one, me myself,
X'd already in my origin,
and not by him.

Non si nasconde fuori
del mondo chi lo salva e non lo sa.
È uno come noi, non dei migliori.

He who saves the world without knowing it
doesn't hide outside the world.
He's someone like us, not one of the best.

Il primo gennaio

So che si può vivere
non esistendo,
emersi da una quinta, da un fondale,
da un fuori che non c'è se mai nessuno
l'ha veduto.
So che si può esistere
non vivendo,
con radici strappate da ogni vento
se anche non muove foglia e non un soffio increspa
l'acqua su cui s'affaccia il tuo salone.
So che non c'è magia
di filtro o d'infusione
che possano spiegare come di te s'azzuffino
dita e capelli, come il tuo riso esploda
nel suo ringraziamento
al minuscolo dio a cui ti affidi,
d'ora in ora diverso, e ne diffidi.
So che mai ti sei posta
il come—il dove—il perché,
pigramente indisposta
al disponibile,
distratta rassegnata al non importa,
al non so quando o quanto, assorta in un oscuro
germinale di larve e arborescenze.
So che quello che afferri,
oggetto o mano, penna o portacenere,
brucia e non se n'accorge,
né te n'avvedi tu animale innocente
inconsapevole
di essere un perno e uno sfacelo, un'ombra
e una sostanza, un raggio che si oscura.
So che si può vivere
nel fuochetto di paglia dell'emulazione

January 1st

I know that life is possible
by not existing,
entering from the wings or backdrop
from a beyond not there if nobody's
ever seen it.
I know that existence is possible
by not living,
roots wrenched up by every wind
though the leaves are still and no breeze
wrinkles the water on which your living room appears.
I know there's no magic,
no philtre or infusion
to explain how your hands and hair
got so tangled, how your laughter explodes
in thanks
to the lowercase god in whom you trust
and distrust since he changes hour by hour.
I know you never posed the questions
why—where—how,
lazily indisposed
to the disponible,
absorbed, resigned to anything at all,
to I don't know when or where, withdrawn in a dark
germinal world of larva and arborescence.
I know that what you grasp,
object or hand, ashtray or pen,
burns unobserved,
and you, innocent animal, take no notice,
unaware
of being pivot and ruin, shade
or substance, a ray of light darkened.
I know one can live
in the small straw-fire of emulation

senza che dalla tua fronte dispaia il segno timbrato
da Chi volle tu fossi . . . e se ne pentì.
                                        Ora
uscita sul terrazzo, annaffi i fiori, scuoti
lo scheletro dell'albero di Natale,
ti accompagna in sordina il mangianastri,
torni dentro, allo specchio ti dispiaci,
ti getti a terra, con lo straccio scrosti
dal pavimento le orme degl'intrusi.
Erano tanti e il più impresentabile
di tutti perché gli altri almeno parlano,
io, a bocca chiusa.

preserving the sign stamped on your brow by Him
who wanted you to be . . . and you regretted it.

                                              Now
outside on your terrace, you water the flowers, shake
the skeleton of the Christmas tree, to the sound
of the tape recorder softly playing,
then return, look disapprovingly in the mirror,
drop to your knees, and scrub the floor
clean of mud tracked in by intruders.
They were numerous and, since the others
at least talked, the most unpresentable
was me, dead silent.

Rebecca

Ogni giorno di più mi scopro difettivo:
manca il totale.
Gli addendi sono a posto, ineccepibili,
ma la somma?
Rebecca abbeverava i suoi cammelli
e anche se stessa.
Io attendo alla penna e alla gamella
per me e per altri.
Rebecca era assetata, io famelico,
ma non saremo assolti.
Non c'era molt'acqua nell'uadi, forse qualche pozzanghera,
e nella mia cucina poca legna da ardere.
Eppure abbiamo tentato per noi, per tutti, nel fumo,
nel fango con qualche vivente bipede o anche quadrupede.
O mansueta Rebecca che non ho mai incontrata!
Appena una manciata di secoli ci dividono,
un batter d'occhio per chi comprende la tua lezione.
Solo il divino è totale nel sorso e nella briciola.
Solo la morte lo vince se chiede l'intera porzione.

Rebecca

Every day I find myself coming up short:
I'm missing the total.
The items to be added are perfectly right,
but the overall total?
Rebecca watered her camels
and herself too.
I attend to pen and messkit
for myself and for others.
Rebecca was thirsty, I'm starved,
but we won't be absolved.
There wasn't much water in the wadi, a few puddles maybe,
and not much kindling in my kitchen either.
Still, for ourselves, for everyone, we tried, in smoke,
in mud, with a few live bipeds or even quadrupeds.
O meek Rebecca whom I never met!
Hardly a handful of centuries divides us,
the twinkling of an eye for those who grasp your teaching.
Only the divine is total in sip and crumb.
Only death triumphs when you ask for both.

Nel silenzio

Oggi è sciopero generale.
Nella strada non passa nessuno.
Solo una radiolina dall'altra parte del muro.
Da qualche giorno deve abitarci qualcuno.
Mi chiedo che ne sarà della produzione.
La primavera stessa tarda alquanto a prodursi.
Hanno spento in anticipo il termosifone.
Si sono accorti ch'è inutile il servizio postale.
Non è gran male il ritardo delle funzioni normali.
È d'obbligo che qualche ingranaggio non ingrani.
Anche i morti si sono messi in agitazione.
Anch'essi fanno parte del silenzio totale.
Tu stai sotto una lapide. Risvegliarti non vale
perché sei sempre desta. Anche oggi ch'è sonno
universale.

In Silence

General strike today.
Deserted streets, no noise.
Only a transistor the other side of the wall:
someone must have moved in a few days ago.
I wonder if production will fall.
This year even spring is late in producing.
They turned off the central heating in anticipation.
They noticed that the postal system wasn't working.
It's no disaster, this suspension of normal operations.
And inevitably a few gears aren't engaged.
Even the dead have started agitating.
They're part of the total silence too.
You're underground. No point arousing you,
you're always awake. Even today,
in the universal sleep.

Luci e colori

Se mai ti mostri hai sempre la liseuse rossa,
gli occhi un po' gonfi come di chi ha veduto.
Sembrano inesplicabili queste tue visite mute.
Probabilmente è solo un lampeggio di lenti,
quasi una gibigianna che tagli la foschia.
L'ultima volta c'era sul scendiletto
colore di albicocca un vermiciattolo
che arrancava a disagio. Non riuscì facile farlo
slittare su un pezzo di carta e buttarlo giù vivo
nel cortile. Tu stessa non devi pesare di più.

Lights and Colors

Whenever you show up, it's always
in that red bed jacket of yours, your eyes
slightly puffy, like those of someone who has seen.
Your silent visits have no apparent explanation.
It could be a glint from your glasses,
some sort of flash slicing the blur.
Last time it was an ugly apricot-colored worm
struggling across the bedside rug. It wasn't easy,
scooping it up on a piece of paper and tossing it,
still wiggling, to the courtyard below.
You couldn't have weighed much more yourself.

Il grillo di Strasburgo notturno col suo trapano
in una crepa della cattedrale;
la Maison Rouge e il barman tuo instillatore di basco,
Ruggero zoppicante e un poco alticcio;
Striggio d'incerta patria, beccatore
di notizie e antipasti, tradito da una turca
(arrubinato il naso di pudore
ove ne fosse cenno, occhio distorto
da non più differibile addition)
ti riapparvero *allora*? Forse nugae
anche minori. Ma tu dicesti solo
«prendi il sonnifero», l'ultima
tua parola—e per me.

The Strasbourg cricket drilling away at night
in a chink of the cathedral;
the Maison Rouge and the bartender Ruggero,
your tutor in Basque, wobbly and a bit tipsy;
and Striggio, of uncertain nationality,
gobbling gossip and antipasti,
betrayed by a Turkish woman (his nose
rosy red with shame at the slightest allusion
to the fact, his eye twisting away
from the no longer deferable *addition*),
did they appear to you *then?* Maybe still smaller
trifles. But all you said was,
"Take a sleeping pill," your last
words—and spoken for me.

L'Altro

Non so chi se n'accorga
ma i nostri commerci con l'Altro
furono un lungo inghippo. Denunziarli
sarà, più che un atto d'ossequio, un impetrare clemenza.
Non siamo responsabili di non essere lui
né ha colpa lui, o merito, della nostra parvenza.
Non c'è neppure timore. Astuto il flamengo nasconde
il capo sotto l'ala e crede che il cacciatore
non lo veda.

The Other

I don't know if it's been observed
but our dealings with the Other
were one long scam. Reporting the fact
wouldn't be deference so much as a plea for mercy.
We can't be faulted for not being Him,
and He deserves no blame, or credit, for our appearance.
We're not even afraid of Him. The flamingo's shrewd:
he buries his head beneath his wing, thinking
the hunter can't spot him.

Notes

The following notes are based in part upon Montale's own comments. Like every present and future translator of Montale, I am indebted to Rosanna Bettarini and Gianfranco Contini, the editors of E. M.'s complete poetic works, *Eugenio Montale/L'opera in versi* (Turin, 1980), which contains both variant drafts and E. M.'s notes to successive editions of the book as well as relevant correspondence, interviews, and essays. I have also cited passages bearing on E. M.'s individual and general poetic practice from the poet's critical essays, principally those gathered in *Sulla poesia* (Milan, 1976).

Interpretive studies of E. M.'s poetry have proliferated in recent years, not only in Italy but throughout Europe and America. No serious translator of the poetry can perform his task without consulting the better Italian critics, above all D'Arco Silvio Avalle, Gianfranco Contini, Marco Forti, Angelo Jacomuzzi, Silvio Ramat, Gilberto Lonardi, Romano Luperini, Vincenzo Mengaldo, Sergio Solmi, and Alvaro Valentini. And in the last decade a number of perceptive studies of E. M. have appeared in America and Britain. These have the merit of drawing upon the best Italian work and qualifying it significantly by the inevitable shift of national and critical focus, and are readily accessible to the reader without Italian. Those on whom I have relied most heavily, and whose work I have cited most frequently, even when I disagree, include:

Almansi, Guido, and Merry, Bruce. *Eugenio Montale / The Private Language of Poetry*. Edinburgh, Scotland, 1977.

Cambon, Glauco. *Eugenio Montale's Poetry / A Dream in Reason's Presence*. Princeton, N.J., 1982.

Cary, Joseph. *Three Modern Italian Poets / Saba, Ungaretti, Montale*. New York, N.Y., 1969; 2nd edition, revised and enlarged, Chicago, 1993.

Huffman, Claire de C. L. *Montale and the Occasions of Poetry*. Princeton, N.J., 1983.

West, Rebecca J. *Eugenio Montale / Poet on the Edge*. Cambridge, Mass., 1981.

I am also indebted to E. M.'s French translator, Patrice Angelini. Even while I often differ in interpretation of details (inevitable when dealing with a poet as difficult and elusive as E. M.), Angelini's attentive concern for the poet's meaning provided a check against the mindsets that often bedevil translators.

E. M.'s own notes and self-commentary have been indicated throughout by the use of the initials E. M.

"Xenia I, 3" (p. 13)

the fake Byzantium of your Venetian / hotel: the Hotel Danieli.

"Xenia 1, 4" (p. 15)

We'd worked out a whistle . . .
    E. M.: "Whistle—a sign of recognition . . ."
    "[That whistle] was no poetic invention. We really worked it out. Later, however, I realized it was all a big mistake. If someone's dead, there's no body. In order to whistle, you need a body." (E. M., in Nascimbeni, p. 73).

"Xenia I, 10" (p. 17)

St. Hermes' cloakroom: the cloakroom belonging to actors, who are held to be under the protection of the god Hermes (or Mercury).

"Xenia I, 13" (p. 19)

Rachel Jacoff, invoking Joseph Brodsky, has observed that "Xenia I, 13" plays off the scene of the meeting of the Roman poet Statius with Dante the pilgrim and Virgil in *Purgatorio*, xxi. The crucial, closing lines of the canto concern the power of literary homage and the nature of spiritual love between shades. Brodsky sees in the scene an emblem for literary tradition and the key to Montale's poetics. See Joseph Brodsky, "In the Shadow of Dante," *Less Than One* (Farrar Straus & Giroux, 1986) 103. The passage in Dante runs:

Già s'inchinava ad abbraciar li piedi
   al mio dottor, ma el li disse: 'Frate,
   non far, ché tu se' ombra e ombra vedi.'
Ed ei surgendo: 'Or puoi la quantitate
   comprender de l'amor ch'a te mi salda,
   quand'io dismento nostra vanitate,
trattando l'ombre come cosa salda.

("Already he was stooping to embrace my teacher's feet; but he said
to him, 'Brother, do not so, for you are a shade and a shade you see.'
And he, rising, 'Now you may comprehend the measure of the love
that burns in me for you, when I forget our emptiness and treat shades
as solid things.") Translation by Charles Singleton.

W. A. pointed to the meeting of Statius and Virgil in the *Purgatorio*
as an "absent epigraph" for Montale's poem "Voce giunta con le fol-
aghe" ("Voice That Came with the Coots") in his notes to the translation
of Montale's *La bufera e altro* (*The Storm and Other Things*). See Montale,
The Storm and Other Things, trans. William Arrowsmith (New York:
W. W. Norton, 1985) 197. [R. W.].

"Xenia II, 4" (p. 25)

emerging from Mongibello's jaws: i.e., from the furnace of Vulcan. Cf.
Dante, *Inferno, xiv,* 55–56.

The good surgeon Mangàno . . . / the billy club of the Blackshirts: Man-
gàno smiles because he recognizes the mischievous (but untranslatable)
connection Mosca has made between his name and the club *(manganello)*
with which (supplemented by doses of olive oil) the Blackshirts used to
beat and mangle *(manganare, dare il mangano à qualcuno)* those who disa-
greed with them.

"Xenia II, 6" (p. 27)

Inferno: red Lombard wine from Valtellina made from the Nebbiolo
grape. In Milan local wines were commonly peddled door to door by
tradesmen or peasants.

"Xenia II, 8" (p. 28)

Paradiso: sweet or semisweet dessert wine also from Valtellina, produced
by the Fattoria Paradiso.

"Xenia II, 14" (p. 31)

The flood, like the storm in *La bufera,* is both personal and historical, devastating memory as it destroys the past. The objects here have been carefully chosen. It is not, for instance, Western culture that is being swept away in the discretely revealed objects—the wax seal with which Ezra Pound inscribed his copy of *Personae* to E. M., Alain's commentary on Valéry's *Charmes,* etc.—but a late phase of High Modernism. The waters of the flood are only implied in the word *alluvione,* so that "fuel oil and shit" can be specified. The cultural destruction is wrought by industrialization, and the impact of mass society, mass culture, on an Italy unprepared and therefore terribly vulnerable.

Charles du Bos (1882–1939): French literary critic, author of *Byron et le besoin de la fatalité* (1929, 1957); *François Mauriac et le problème du romancier catholique* (1933); *Grandeur et misère de Benjamin Constaut* (1946); and *Le dialogue avec André Gide* (1947), among other works. In E. M.'s Florence during the thirties, DuBos was regarded with something like religious awe.

It's as though the flood had swept away a part of the mind of Europe, above all that part which had attempted, in its own frantic way, to make a dam of literature that would contain the floodwaters. The flood trashes the literary culture of E. M.'s Florence in the thirties. Books become detritus, soiled relics. Pound's ransacking of the past, Alain's monkish efforts to pin Valéry down and thereby save the poet's texts (which he treated as though they were sacred scripture), Campana with his evocations of the Italian past, names of cities, the romanticism of the *poeta germanicus:* piling up fragments, the writers in E. M.'s list all seem, in retrospect, to have had an anticipation of the flood. Campana and Pound end up in lunatic asylums, while DuBos tried frantically to assert an identity through the force of his dedication, as though the memory bank of a decade had been wiped out, erased from history.

Note the "double-padlocked cellar": security precautions necessitated by the phenomenon which Italians in the postwar years increasingly came to feel was the product of *una societá infida,* a society without trust. It is a world controlled by the fear of thieves for whom these cultural objects fetch a good price because "art" is profitable; it sells. The moral courage to resist, to hold on to an identity, is Mosca's great gift to the poet, the domestic product of a life that was *lived,* that was not merely literature:

tough, warm, honest, characterized by what E. M. would later say of his friend Fadin, "daily decency, the hardest of all the virtues."

the wax seal with Ezra's beard: In a postwar piece on Pound (SP449), E. M. wrote that Ezra "used to wear his own likeness carved in the cameo of a large ring, which he used as a seal when dedicating his books." Elsewhere (SP492-3) E. M. adds: "When I made his acquaintance around 1925 . . . his poems were collected in *Personae* which he inscribed for me, stamping it in wax with the cameo of his ring, carved by Gaudier Brzeska."

Alain's Valéry: Emile Auguste Chartier Alain. French critic whose painstakingly exacting gloss on Valéry (*Commentaire à Charmes,* 1930) evidently impressed E. M. with its zealous effort to clarify and decipher Valéry's often extremely elusive meaning.

the Manuscript / of the Orphic Songs: the *Canti orfici* of the Italian poet Dino Campana (1885–1932), which E. M. possessed in the early (1914) and "extremely poor and inaccurate Marradi edition." (SP348). According to E. M. (SP251 ff.) "the idea of a poetry—'European, musical, colorful' in Campana was not only instinctive but a fact of culture, . . . an Orphic poetry not limited to the title of his book, and one which cannot be viewed as unrelated to his conviction of himself as a late Germanic rhapsode lured and blinded by the passionate lights of the Mediterranean . . . Like the early Di Chirico, Campana also suggestively evokes the ancient Italian cities; Bologna, Faenza, Florence, Genoa blaze through his poems and spark some of his loftiest moments."

"The Euphrates" (p. 147)

Who knows what you'll have seen . . . . : the "you" is Clizia.

"The Arno at Rovezzano" (p. 149)

Still another poem of musing reminiscence. In his explanation to Silvio Guarnieri, E. M. identified the "you" of the poem as a girl courted by the economist and sociologist, Achille Loria. As an abbess, her convent name was Sister Jerome, her worldly name Baroness Von Agel. See Lorenzo Greco, *Montale commenta Montale*. (Parma: Pratiche Editrice, 1980) 65. [R.W.].

"*Toi qui fais l'endormie*": sardonic serenade from Act IV of Gounod's *Faust,* presumably sung by Mephistopheles-Montale on behalf of Faust-

Loria to Marguerite-Baroness Von Agel aka Sister Jerome. E. M. has slightly adapted the words of the original: "Vous qui faites l'endormie."

"Ex Voto" (p. 159)

I insist / on seeking you . . . E. M.: "I can't give a [single woman's] name [to that 'you']. It's a figurative representation, a fantasia." For the image of woman as shoot or greening plant, see "Chrysalis" in *Cuttlefish Bones:* "These are yours, these scattered / trees, moist, joyous, / revived by April's breath. / For me in this shadow observing you, / another shoot greens again—and you *are*."
    if your fate brims, overflowing mine. See "Delta" in *Cuttlefish Bones.*

"I Came into the World . . ." (p. 163)

Alma Mater was asleep. "Alma Mater," according to E. M.'s note, means "Nationalism."

"Piròpo, in Conclusion" (p. 179)

This poem is omitted from the sequence "After a Flight" in the standard edition of Montale's collected poems, *L'Opera in versi,* ed. Rosanna Bettarini and Gianfranco Contini (Turin: Einaudi, 1980). But the editors have included it in an appendix, along with some elucidating comments by the poet. In a letter to Luciano Rebay, E. M. explained that "*piròpos* are those gallant remarks which all men toss out at the women they meet on the street. All the women appreciate them . . ." Writing in 1978 to Rosanna Bettarini, E. M. declared the *"Piròpo"* to be a "thorny" question: "The sequence 'After a Flight' is not, strictly speaking, an erotic poem; it becomes one however essentially when the old man returns definitively to a childlike state. Perhaps it would be a good idea . . . if worst comes to worst, to place it in a note: placed where?" Writing to Rebay in 1970, E. M. had identified *"Piròpo"* as the ninth poem in the sequence: "The climax comes at the seventh, then follows the denial and finally the bitter-joking farewell. That's how it strikes me . . ."
    In "Commento a se stesso" E. M. explained, "The 'suite' is the story of a last love between a young woman and an old man. The girl was subject to recurrent depressions which approached madness."
    These notes are included in *L'Opera in versi,* 1035–1036. I have translated them. [R.W.].

"Without Safe-Conduct" (p. 189)

Hannah Kahn; a Jewish woman who, as an American, was apparently in no real danger. "She came to see me," said E. M., "claiming to be a friend of Clizia [Irma Brandeis]." At the time (1944), E. M. had taken refuge from the retreating German troops in a cellar in Florence. Later, he received an article written by Hannah Kahn and realized that she had escaped the gas chamber.

talked to me about you: the "you" is Clizia.

on the Scarpuccia / or the Costa San Giorgio, the place of the golden idol: Scarpuccia and Costa San Giorgio are the sites of well-known Florentine promenades along and above the steep slopes rising uphill from the Arno and Porta San Giorgio. For the mysterious "golden idol," see "Costa San Giorgio" in *The Occasions* and note thereon.

"In Silence" (p. 207)

You're underground. No point arousing you: the "you" is Mosca, in her grave at Ema. See "It's Raining."

"Lights and Colors," (p. 209)

Whenever you show up: the "you" is, once again, Mosca.

"The Strasbourg cricket drilling away . . ." (p. 211)

your tutor in Basque: the "you" is Mosca.

and Striggio, of uncertain nationality: Striggio is actually Bigio, a free-lance writer (and mooch) whose name has been mischievously deformed, *more ovo,* by Mosca: Striggio appears to be a play on *strige* (owl, witch) or *striggine* (sorcerer).

"The Other" (p. 213)

The Other: that is, *Altrui,* Dante's word for God, the absolute Otherness.